Writing the Critical Essay

Stem Cell Research

An OPPOSING VIEWPOINTS® Guide

Lauri S. Friedman, *Book Editor*

OPPOSING
VIEWPOINTS®
SERIES

GREENHAVEN PRESS
A part of Gale, Cengage Learning

GALE
CENGAGE Learning

Detroit • New York • San Francisco • New Haven, Conn • Waterville, Maine • London

Christine Nasso, *Publisher*
Elizabeth Des Chenes, *Managing Editor*

© 2011 Greenhaven Press, a part of Gale, Cengage Learning

Gale and Greenhaven Press are registered trademarks used herein under license.

For more information, contact:
Greenhaven Press
27500 Drake Rd.
Farmington Hills, MI 48331-3535
Or you can visit our Internet site at gale.cengage.com

For product information and technology assistance, contact us at

Gale Customer Support, 1-800-877-4253
For permission to use material from this text or product, submit all requests online at
www.cengage.com/permissions

Further permissions questions can be e-mailed to permissionrequest@cengage.com

Articles in Greenhaven Press anthologies are often edited for length to meet page requirements. In addition, original titles of these works are changed to clearly present the main thesis and to explicitly indicate the author's opinion. Every effort is made to ensure that Greenhaven Press accurately reflects the original intent of the authors. Every effort has been made to trace the owners of copyrighted material.

Cover image © Sandy Huffaker/Corbis.

LIBRARY OF CONGRESS CATALOGING-IN-PUBLICATION DATA

Stem cell research / Lauri S. Friedman, book editor.
   p. cm. -- (Writing the critical essay: An opposing viewpoints guide)
  Includes bibliographical references and index.
  ISBN 978-0-7377-5025-6 (hardcover)
  1. Stem cells--Juvenile literature. 2. Embryonic stem cells--Juvenile literature. I. Friedman, Lauri S.
  QH588.S83S7393 2011
  174.2'8--dc22
                                        2010030906

Printed in the United States of America
1 2 3 4 5 6 7 14 13 12 11 10

CONTENTS

Examining the state of writing and how it is taught in the United States was the official purpose of the National Commission on Writing in America's Schools and Colleges. The commission, made up of teachers, school administrators, business leaders, and college and university presidents, released its first report in 2003. "Despite the best efforts of many educators," commissioners argued, "writing has not received the full attention it deserves." Among the findings of the commission was that most fourth-grade students spent less than three hours a week writing, that three-quarters of high school seniors never receive a writing assignment in their history or social studies classes, and that more than 50 percent of first-year students in college have problems writing error-free papers. The commission called for a "cultural sea change" that would increase the emphasis on writing for both elementary and secondary schools. These conclusions have made some educators realize that writing must be emphasized in the curriculum. As colleges are demanding an ever-higher level of writing proficiency from incoming students, schools must respond by making students more competent writers. In response to these concerns, the SAT, an influential standardized test used for college admissions, required an essay for the first time in 2005.

Books in the Writing the Critical Essay: An Opposing Viewpoints Guide series use the patented Opposing Viewpoints format to help students learn to organize ideas and arguments and to write essays using common critical writing techniques. Each book in the series focuses on a particular type of essay writing—including expository, persuasive, descriptive, and narrative—that students learn while being taught both the five-paragraph essay as well as longer pieces of writing that have an opinionated focus. These guides include everything necessary to help students research, outline, draft, edit, and ultimately write successful essays across the curriculum, including essays for the SAT.

Using Opposing Viewpoints

This series is inspired by and builds upon Greenhaven Press's acclaimed Opposing Viewpoints series. As in the parent series, each book in the Writing the Critical Essay series focuses on a timely and controversial social issue that provides lots of opportunities for creating thought-provoking essays. The first section of each volume begins with a brief introductory essay that provides context for the opposing viewpoints that follow. These articles are chosen for their accessibility and clearly stated views. The thesis of each article is made explicit in the article's title and is accentuated by its pairing with an opposing or alternative view. These essays are both models of persuasive writing techniques and valuable research material that students can mine to write their own informed essays. Guided reading and discussion questions help lead students to key ideas and writing techniques presented in the selections.

The second section of each book begins with a preface discussing the format of the essays and examining characteristics of the featured essay type. Model five-paragraph and longer essays then demonstrate that essay type. The essays are annotated so that key writing elements and techniques are pointed out to the student. Sequential, step-by-step exercises help students construct and refine thesis statements; organize material into outlines; analyze and try out writing techniques; write transitions, introductions, and conclusions; and incorporate quotations and other researched material. Ultimately, students construct their own compositions using the designated essay type.

The third section of each volume provides additional research material and writing prompts to help the student. Additional facts about the topic of the book serve as a convenient source of supporting material for essays. Other features help students go beyond the book for their research. Like other Greenhaven Press books, each book in the Writing the Critical Essay series includes bibliographic listings of relevant periodical articles, books, Web sites, and organizations to contact.

Writing the Critical Essay: An Opposing Viewpoints Guide will help students master essay techniques that can be used in any discipline.

To Fund or Not to Fund?

Stem cell research is expensive, and whether the government should help pay for it has been a long-standing part of the controversies surrounding it. The presidential administrations of the early twenty-first century have taken dramatically different positions on whether the government should fund embryonic stem cell research, and each has been met with varying forms of opposition.

Early in his first term, on August 9, 2001, President George W. Bush decided to limit the amount of money the government could put toward stem cell research involving human embryos. Bush worried about the research's morality: an ardently pro-life president, Bush claimed that research on embryos amounted to the taking of life for scientific gain, something that he could not in good conscience support. Bush also worried that unbridled stem cell research would result in human cloning, immoral experimentation, and the general devaluation of human life. "Embryonic stem cell research is at the leading edge of a series of moral hazards," he said. "While we're all hopeful about the potential of this research, no one can be certain that the science will live up to the hope it has generated."[1]

Therefore, one of Bush's first acts in office was to sign an executive order that banned the use of federal funds on new stem cell lines. Federal money could be put toward stem cell research only if the research was done on the few dozen stem cell lines that were already in existence at the time of the ban, since, as Bush put it, "the life-or-death decision has already been made."[2]

But limiting federal funding to these few lines was problematic for several reasons. First, several of the lines soon became contaminated with foreign cells that made research on them difficult or inaccurate. Second, there were not enough stem cell lines to go around to the thousands of scientists and laboratories who wanted access to them. For these reasons, many claimed that restrictions on federal funding were preventing the discovery of treatments and cures for some of America's worst diseases. In addition, America risked losing some of its best scientists to other countries because they could not get funding to perform their research. Meanwhile, research was being conducted by unregulated private firms, making its quality and methodology questionable.

Democratic senator Barbara Mikulski was one person who worried that the Bush Administration's approach to stem cell research was damaging both to America's international reputation and to sick Americans awaiting cures. "That's another patient who may have been saved, another family that may not have to watch a loved one suffer," she said. "Scientists have their hands tied behind their backs. Cell lines that can be used for research now are deficient and defective. . . . This goes against the way science is studied, slowing down potential breakthroughs. Our country is sitting back while other countries are moving forward."[3]

Like his predecessor, Barack Obama made stem cell research an early priority of his presidency when he took office in 2009. However, Obama had a fundamentally different view of embryonic stem cell research. He too opposed human cloning and believed in the importance of conducting ethical scientific research. But like Mikulski, Obama thought the Bush ban on funding stifled the potential for discovery and the United States' position as an international leader in scientific discovery. As he put it:

> Medical miracles do not happen simply by accident. They result from painstaking and costly research— from years of lonely trial and error, much of which never bears fruit—and from a government willing to support that work. From life-saving vaccines, to pioneering cancer treatments, to the sequencing

of the human genome—that is the story of scientific progress in America. When government fails to make these investments, opportunities are missed. Promising avenues go unexplored. Some of our best scientists leave for other countries that will sponsor their work. And those countries may surge ahead of ours in the advances that transform our lives.[4]

Therefore, on March 9, 2009, Obama lifted the Bush Administration ban, allowing funding to be applied to the creation of new stem cell lines and to work on lines that had been created under the sponsorship of private companies or without federal funding.

Obama's decision to return federal funding to embryonic stem cell research proved to be nearly as controversial as Bush's decision to withdraw it. Long-time opponents of stem cell research contended that embryonic stem cell research is inherently immoral since it destroys embryos and employs procedures that could in theory be used to clone humans. Others, like columnist Bob Kemp, argued that funding should be given to less controversial and potentially more productive stem cell research techniques that involve adult cells or cells made from human skin. "If you want to stop government waste, embryonic stem cell research is a good place to start," said Kemp. "Over $3 billion dollars has already been allocated for this bottomless pit which holds no promise of doing anything but sucking more and more money out of the federal budget each year."[5]

Yet polls reveal the majority of the American public supports the Obama decision, at least for now. A May 2009 Gallup poll found that 57 percent of Americans consider medical research using stem cells obtained from human embryos to be morally acceptable. A different Gallup poll taken just after Obama announced his decision to reverse the Bush ban on funding revealed that only 4 in 10 Americans favored keeping the Bush restrictions— the majority of respondents said they supported easing restrictions, or eliminating restrictions entirely.

Clearly, even as federal policies on embryonic stem cell research have changed, controversy over its morality remains. It seems certain that scientists, politicians, religious leaders, philosophers, and others will continue to debate whether this research should be pursued, who should fund it, and what benefits it offers. To this end, *Writing the Critical Essay: An Opposing Viewpoints Guide: Stem Cell Research* exposes readers to arguments made about stem cell research and helps them develop tools to craft their own expository essays on the subject.

Notes

1. CNN.com, "President George W. Bush's Address on Stem Cell Research," August 9, 2001. http://archives.cnn.com/2001/ALLPOLITICS/08/09/bush.transcript.
2. CNN.com, "President George W. Bush's Address on Stem Cell Research."
3. Barbara A. Mikulski, "Stem Cell Research Is About Saving Lives, Not Party Lines," April 11, 2007. http://mikulski.senate.gov/record.cfm?id = 272200.
4. Barack Obama, "Remarks of President Barack Obama—as Prepared for Delivery, Signing of Stem Cell Executive Order and Scientific Integrity Presidential Memorandum, March 9, 2009. www.whitehouse.gov/the_press_office/remarks-of-the-president-as-prepared-for-delivery-signing-of-stem-cell-executive-order-and-scientific-integrity-presidential-memorandum.
5. Bob Kemp, "Embryonic Stem Cell Research: Bad Science Funded by the White House," Renew America.com, July 30, 2009. www.renewamerica.com/columns/kemp/090730.

Section One:
Opposing
Viewpoints
on Stem Cell
Research

Using Embryos for Stem Cell Research Is Moral

Michael J. Sandel, interview by Stem Cell Lines

In the following essay *Stem Cell Lines* interviews Michael J. Sandel who argues it is moral to use embryos for stem cell research. In his opinion, embryos are only potential human beings—if left to develop they will become human beings, but until then they should not be given the same status as human persons. While humans develop from embryos, Sandel says embryos themselves are different. He explains that an embryo is a simple group of cells in the earliest stage of human development, but this is very different from being a human, or even a baby, because embryos are incapable of experiencing life the way humans at the infant, child, or even adult stages do. For example, embryos do not yet have consciousness, are incapable of feeling emotions or physical sensations, and do not possess other qualities that make humans human. These qualities develop over time, as an embryo matures into an infant. For all of these reasons, Sandel criticizes those who equate embryos with humans. He concludes they hinder the biomedical promise of stem cell research and threaten countless human lives in the process.

Sandel is a professor of government at Harvard University.

"Examining the Ethics of Embryonic Stem Cell Research: A Conversation with HSCI's Michael J. Sandel," *HSCI*, June 19, 2007. Reproduced by permission of Harvard Stem Cell Institute.

Consider the following questions:

1. How many cells make up a blastocyst, according to Sandel?
2. In what way are embryos and humans like acorns and oak trees, according to the author?
3. Sandel discusses the status of the 400,000 excess embryos in U.S. fertility clinics. In his opinion, what does the status of these embryos reveal about the morality of stem cell research?

[*Stem Cell Lines*] Q. What are the main arguments for and against embryonic stem cell research?

[Michael Sandel] A. Proponents argue that embryonic stem cell research holds great promise for understanding and curing diabetes, Parkinson's disease, spinal cord injury, and other debilitating conditions. Opponents argue that the research is unethical, because deriving the stem cells destroys the blastocyst, an unimplanted human embryo at the sixth to eighth day of development. As [President George W.] Bush declared when he vetoed last year's [2006] stem cell bill, the federal government should not support "the taking of innocent human life."

It is surprising that, despite the extensive public debate—in Congress, during the 2004 and 2006 election campaigns, and on the Sunday morning talk shows— relatively little attention has been paid to the moral issue at the heart of the controversy: Are the opponents of stem cell research correct in their claim that the unimplanted human embryo is already a human being, morally equivalent to a person?

The Truth About Blastocysts

Q. Considering that the moral and political controversy over embryonic stem cell research centers on this very

Activists gather at the U.S. Capitol Building to promote the morality of embryonic stem cell research.

question, why do you think there is so little attention being paid to it?

A. Perhaps this claim has gone unaddressed because stem cell proponents and many in the media consider it obviously false—a faith-based belief that no rational argument could possibly dislodge. If so, they are making a mistake. The fact that a moral belief may be rooted in religious conviction neither exempts it from challenge nor puts it beyond the realm of public debate. Ignoring the claim that the blastocyst is a person fails to respect those who oppose embryonic stem cell research on principled moral grounds. It has also led the media to miss glaring contradictions in Bush's stem cell policy, which does not actually live up to the principle it invokes—that destroying an embryo is like killing a child.

Q. What are the contradictions in Bush's stance?

A. Before we address that, it is important to be clear about the embryo from which stem cells are extracted.

It is not implanted and growing in a woman's uterus. It is not a fetus. It has no recognizable human features or form.

It is, rather, a blastocyst, a cluster of 180 to 200 cells, growing in a petri dish, barely visible to the naked eye. Such blastocysts are either cloned in the lab or created in fertility clinics. The bill recently passed by Congress would fund stem cell research only on excess blastocysts left over from infertility treatments.

The blastocyst represents such an early stage of embryonic development that the cells it contains have not yet differentiated, or taken on the properties of particular organs or tissues—kidneys, muscles, spinal cord, and so on. This is why the stem cells that are extracted from the blastocyst hold the promise of developing, with proper coaxing in the lab, into any kind of cell the researcher wants to study or repair.

The Root of the Controversy

The moral and political controversy arises from the fact that extracting the stem cells destroys the blastocyst. It is important to grasp the full force of the claim that the embryo is morally equivalent to a person, a fully developed human being.

For those who hold this view, extracting stem cells from a blastocyst is as morally abhorrent as harvesting organs from a baby to save other people's lives. This is the position of Senator Sam Brownback, Republican of Kansas, a leading advocate of the right-to-life position. In Brownback's view, "a human embryo . . . is a human being just like you and me; and it deserves the same respect that our laws give to us all."

If Brownback is right, then embryonic stem cell research is immoral because it amounts to killing a person to treat other people's diseases.

Q. What is the basis for the belief that personhood begins at conception?

A. Some base this belief on the religious conviction that the soul enters the body at the moment of conception. Others defend it without recourse to religion, by the following line of reasoning: Human beings are not things. Their lives must not be sacrificed against their will, even for the sake of good ends, like saving other people's lives. The reason human beings must not be treated as things is that they are inviolable. At what point do humans acquire this inviolability? The answer cannot depend on the age or developmental stage of a particular human life. Infants are

The Majority of Americans Think Stem Cell Research Is Moral

Since 2003 increasing numbers of Americans have considered the use of embryos in stem cell research to be a moral endeavor.

Question: "Do you think it is morally acceptable or morally wrong to conduct medical research using stem cells obtained from human embryos?"

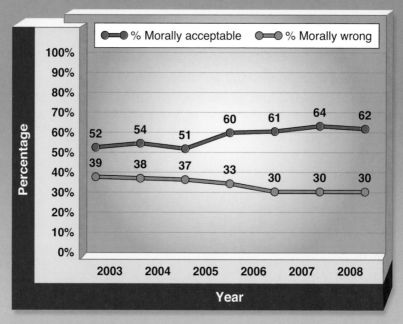

Taken from: "Majority of Americans Likely Support Stem Cell Decision," Gallup Organization, March 9, 2009. www.gallup.com/poll/116485/Majority-Americans-Likely-Support-Stem-Cell-Decision.aspx.

inviolable, and few people would countenance harvesting organs for transplantation even from a fetus.

Every human being—each one of us—began life as an embryo. Unless we can point to a definitive moment in the passage from conception to birth that marks the emergence of the human person, we must regard embryos as possessing the same inviolability as fully developed human beings.

The Difference Between Embryos and Persons

Q. By this line of reasoning, human embryos are inviolable and should not be used for research, even if that research might save many lives.

A. Yes, but this argument can be challenged on a number of grounds. First, it is undeniable that a human embryo is "human life" in the biological sense that it is living rather than dead, and human rather than, say, bovine.

But this biological fact does not establish that the blastocyst is a human being, or a person. Any living human cell (a skin cell, for example) is "human life" in the sense of being human rather than bovine and living rather than dead. But no one would consider a skin cell a person, or deem it inviolable. Showing that a blastocyst is a human being, or a person, requires further argument.

Some try to base such an argument on the fact that human beings develop from embryo to fetus to child. Every person was once an embryo, the argument goes, and there is no clear, non-arbitrary line between conception and adulthood that can tell us when personhood begins. Given the lack of such a line, we should regard the blastocyst as a person, as morally equivalent to a fully developed human being.

Embryos Are *Potential* Human Beings

Q. What is the flaw in this argument?

A. Consider an analogy: although every oak tree was once an acorn, it does not follow that acorns are oak trees, or that I should treat the loss of an acorn eaten by a squirrel in my front yard as the same kind of loss as the death of an oak tree felled by a storm. Despite their developmental continuity, acorns and oak trees differ. So do human embryos and human beings, and in the same way. Just as acorns are potential oaks, human embryos are potential human beings.

The distinction between a potential person and an actual one makes a moral difference. Sentient creatures make claims on us that nonsentient ones do not; beings capable of experience and consciousness make higher claims still. Human life develops by degrees.

Q. Yet there are people who disagree that life develops by degrees and believe that a blastocyst is a person and, therefore, morally equivalent to a fully developed human being.

A. Certainly some people hold this belief. But a reason to be skeptical of the notion that blastocysts are persons is to notice that many who invoke it do not embrace its full implications.

President Bush is a case in point. In 2001, he announced a policy that restricted federal funding to already existing stem cell lines, so that no taxpayer funds would encourage or support the destruction of embryos. And in 2006, he vetoed a bill that would have funded new embryonic stem cell research, saying that he did not want to support "the taking of innocent human life."

But it is a striking feature of the president's position that, while restricting the funding of embryonic stem cell research, he has made no effort to ban it. To adapt a slogan from the [Bill] Clinton administration, the Bush policy might be summarized as "don't fund, don't ban." But this policy is at odds with the notion that embryos are human beings.

A Hypocritical Position

Q. If Bush's policy were consistent with his stated beliefs, how, in your opinion, would it differ from his current "don't fund, don't ban" policy?

A. If harvesting stem cells from a blastocyst were truly on a par with harvesting organs from a baby, then the morally responsible policy would be to ban it, not merely deny it federal funding.

If some doctors made a practice of killing children to get organs for transplantation, no one would take the position that the infanticide should be ineligible for federal funding but allowed to continue in the private sector. In fact, if we were persuaded that embryonic stem cell research were tantamount to infanticide, we would not only ban it but treat it as a grisly form of murder and subject scientists who performed it to criminal punishment. . . .

Q. You have stated that the president's refusal to ban privately funded embryonic stem cell research is not the only way in which his policies betray the principle that embryos are persons. How so?

A. In the course of treating infertility, American fertility clinics routinely discard thousands of human embryos. The bill that recently passed in the Senate would

The author believes that a distinction between potential humans (embryos) and actual humans makes a moral difference when it comes to stem cell research.

It Is Moral to Use Discarded Embryos in Stem Cell Research

Some stem cell research can be conducted using human embryos from fertility clinics. These are embryos that were created for the purpose of implanting them into a woman who has difficulty getting pregnant on her own, but for a variety of reasons end up unused. The majority of Americans say that if these embryos are going to be discarded anyway, they would rather see them used for research.

Question: "There is a type of medical research that involves using special cells, called embryonic stem cells, that might be used in the future to treat or cure many diseases, such as Alzheimer's, Parkinson's, diabetes, and spinal cord injury. It involves using human embryos discarded from fertility clinics that no longer need them. Some people say that using human embryos for research is wrong. Do you favor or oppose using discarded embryos to conduct stem cell research to try to find cures for the diseases I mentioned?"

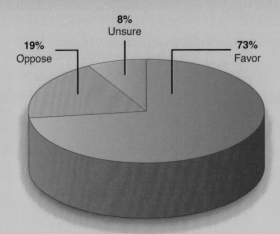

8%
Unsure

19%
Oppose

73%
Favor

Taken from: *Time*, June 18–25, 2008.

fund stem cell research only on these excess embryos, which are already bound for destruction. (This is also the position taken by former [Massachsetts] governor Mitt Romney, who supports stem cell research on embryos left over from fertility clinics.) Although Bush would ban the use of such embryos in federally funded research, he has not called for legislation to ban the creation and destruction of embryos by fertility clinics.

Logical Inconsistencies Reveal the Morality of Stem Cell Research

Q. If embryos are morally equivalent to fully developed human beings, doesn't it then follow that allowing fertility clinics to discard thousands of embryos is condoning mass murder?

A. It does. If embryos are human beings, to allow fertility clinics to discard them is to countenance, in effect, the widespread creation and destruction of surplus children. Those who believe that a blastocyst is morally equivalent to a baby must believe that the 400,000 excess embryos languishing in freezers in U.S. fertility clinics are like newborns left to die by exposure on a mountainside. But those who view embryos in this way should not only be opposing embryonic stem cell research; they should also be leading a campaign to shut down what they must regard as rampant infanticide in fertility clinics.

Some principled right-to-life opponents of stem cell research meet this test of moral consistency. Bush's "don't fund, don't ban" policy does not. Those who fail to take seriously the belief that embryos are persons miss this point. Rather than simply complain that the president's stem cell policy allows religion to trump science, critics should ask why the president does not pursue the full implications of the principle he invokes.

If he does not want to ban embryonic stem cell research, or prosecute stem cell scientists for murder, or ban fertility clinics from creating and discarding excess

> ## Renewed Hope for Cures
>
> [In 2009] President Barack Obama signed an executive order lifting the nation's ban on funding research on new embryonic stem cell lines. With it, there is new hope for millions of diabetes sufferers, including me, as well as millions more suffering from other debilitating diseases. This isn't just a symbolic gesture—it's a move that actually enables the greatest scientists in our country to get back to work on finding cures.
>
> Joe Trippi, "Science You Can Believe In," RealClear-Politics, March 13, 2009. www.realclearpolitics.com/articles/2009/03/science_you_can_believe_in.html.

embryos, this must mean that he does not really consider human embryos as morally equivalent to fully developed human beings after all.

But if he doesn't believe that embryos are persons, then why ban federally funded embryonic stem cell research that holds promise for curing diseases and saving lives?

Analyze the essay:

1. Sandel points out what he deems the logical inconsistencies made by those who oppose stem cell research on the grounds that destroying an embryo is morally equivalent to destroying a person. Identify at least two of these inconsistencies.
2. To make his argument, Sandel compares blastocysts with other human tissues such as skin cells. In your opinion, is a blastocyst more like a skin cell or more like a person? Why?

Using Embryos for Stem Cell Research Is Immoral

Committee on Pro-Life Activities of the United States Conference of Catholic Bishops (USCCB)

The Committee on Pro-Life Activities of the United States Conference of Catholic Bishops (USCCB) is an arm of the Catholic Church. In the following essay they argue that using embryos for stem cell research is immoral. The authors explain that stem cell research involves using human stem cells taken from embryos. Even though these embryos are just a few days old, the cells that compose them are still a form of human life, they contend. Because of this, the authors consider stem cell research to be murder because it causes the death of the embryo, which will become a person if left to develop. Although stem cell research can offer cures for many diseases, the authors claim it is unethical to destroy one human for the benefit of another. Since all humans deserve the right to life, the authors conclude that it is unethical to use embryos for stem cell research.

Consider the following questions:

1. What is wrong, in the authors' opinion, with the argument that destroying embryos for stem cell research can save people who suffer from Parkinson's or Alzheimer's disease?
2. Of what group do the authors say embryos are complete and distinct members?
3. What does the Declaration of Independence guarantee all Americans? How does this factor into the authors' argument?

On Embryonic Stem Cell Research. Washington, DC: United States Conference of Catholic Bishops, 2008. © USCCB. All rights reserved. Reproduced by permission.

Stem cell research has captured the imagination of many in our society. Stem cells are relatively unspecialized cells that, when they divide, can replicate themselves and also produce a variety of more specialized cells. Scientists hope these biological building blocks can be directed to produce many types of cells to repair the human body, cure disease, and alleviate suffering. Stem cells from adult tissues, umbilical cord blood, and placenta (often loosely called "adult stem cells") can be obtained without harm to the donor and without any ethical problem, and these have already demonstrated great medical promise. But some scientists are most intrigued by stem cells obtained by destroying an embryonic human being in the first week or so of development. Harvesting these "embryonic stem cells" involves the deliberate killing of innocent human beings, a gravely immoral act. Yet some try to justify it by appealing to a hoped-for future benefit to others.

The Imperative to Respect Human Life

[As stated by Pope Benedict in 2008,] the Catholic Church "appreciates and encourages the progress of the biomedical sciences which open up unprecedented therapeutic prospects." At the same time, it affirms that true service to humanity begins with respect for each and every human life.

Because life is our first and most basic gift from an infinitely loving God, it deserves our utmost respect and protection. Direct attacks on innocent human life are always gravely wrong. Yet some researchers, ethicists, and policy makers claim that we may directly kill innocent embryonic human beings as if they were mere objects of research—and even that we should make taxpayers complicit in such killing through use of public funds. Thus, while human life is threatened in many ways in our society, the destruction of human embryos for stem cell research confronts us with the issue of respect for life in a stark new way.

There Is No "Greater Good" in Death

Almost everyone agrees with the principle that individuals and governments should not attack the lives of innocent human beings. However, several arguments have been used to justify destroying human embryos to obtain stem cells. It has been argued that (1) any harm done in this case is outweighed by the potential benefits; (2) what is destroyed is not a human life, or at least not a human being with fundamental human rights; and (3) dissecting human embryos for their cells should not be seen as involving a loss of embryonic life. We would like to comment briefly on each of these arguments.

First, the false assumption that a good end can justify direct killing has been the source of much evil in our world. This utilitarian ethic has especially disastrous consequences when used to justify lethal experiments on fellow human beings in the name of progress. No commitment to a hoped-for "greater good" can erase or

Protesters outside George Washington University demonstrate against stem cell research, promoting their view that embryos are human lives.

diminish the wrong of directly taking innocent human lives here and now. In fact, policies undermining our respect for human life can only endanger the vulnerable patients that stem cell research offers to help. The same ethic that justifies taking some lives to help the patient with Parkinson's or Alzheimer's disease today can be used to sacrifice that very patient tomorrow, if his or her survival is viewed as disadvantaging other human beings considered more deserving or productive. The suffering of patients and families affected by devastating illness deserves our compassion and our committed response, but not at the cost of our respect for life itself.

Embryos Are People, Too

Second, some claim that the embryo in his or her first week of development is too small, immature, or undeveloped to be considered a "human life." Yet the human embryo, from conception onward, is as much a living member of the human species as any of us. As a matter of biological fact, this new living organism has the full complement of human genes and is actively expressing those genes to live and develop in a way that is unique to human beings, setting the essential foundation for further development. Though dependent in many ways, the embryo is a complete and distinct member of the species *Homo sapiens*, who develops toward maturity by directing his or her own integrated organic functioning. All later stages of life are steps in the history of a human being already in existence. Just as each of us was once an adolescent, a child, a newborn infant, and a child in the womb, each of us was once an embryo.

Others, while acknowledging the scientific fact that the embryo is a living member of the human species, claim that life at this earliest stage is too weak or undeveloped, too lacking in mental or physical abilities, to

A Dangerous Door to Open

Embryonic stem cell research threatens to become a launching pad to an ever-deepening erosion of the unique moral status of human life.

Wesley J. Smith, "Stem Cell Debate Is Over Ethics, Not Science," *Orthodoxy Today*, March 23, 2009. www.orthodoxytoday.org/artciles-2009/ Smith-Stem-Cell-Debate-Is-Over-Ethics-Not-Science.php.

Embryonic Stem Cell Research Destroys Life

Embryonic stem cell research is conducted by destroying cells that if implanted into a woman's uterus would go on to develop into a baby. For this reason, opponents of embryonic stem cell research describe the process as murder—because it often interrupts what would have become a life.

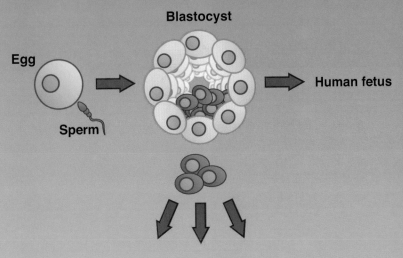

Blastocyst

Egg

Sperm

Human fetus

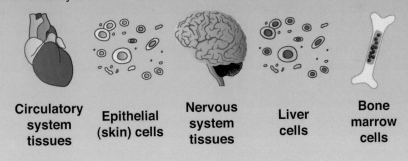

Tissues that can be derived from stem cells harvested from a blastocyst:

Circulatory system tissues	Epithelial (skin) cells	Nervous system tissues	Liver cells	Bone marrow cells

Compiled by editor.

have full human worth or human rights. But to claim that our rights depend on such factors is to deny that human beings have human *dignity*, that we have inherent value simply by being members of the human family. If fundamental rights such as the right to life are based

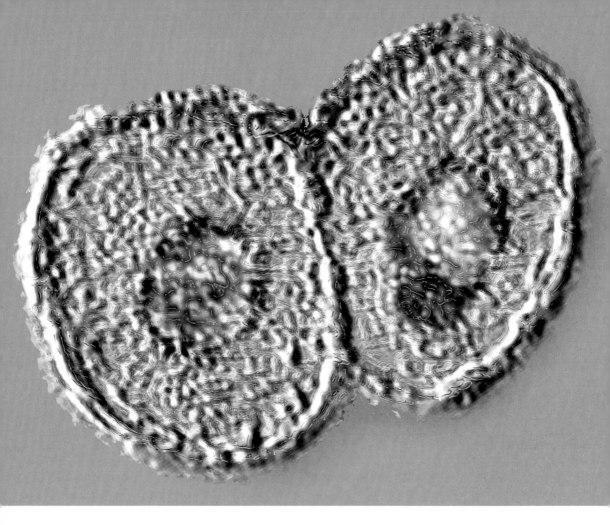

According to the authors, an embryo is a human life, and extracting human embryonic stem cells, like the ones pictured, is unethical.

on abilities or qualities that can appear or disappear, grow or diminish, and be greater or lesser in different human beings, then there are no inherent human rights, no true human equality, only privileges for the strong. As believers who recognize each human life as the gift of an infinitely loving God, we insist that every human being, however small or seemingly insignificant, matters to God—hence everyone, no matter how weak or small, is of concern to us.

America Guarantees the Right to Life

This is not only a teaching of the Catholic Church. Our nation's Declaration of Independence took for granted that human beings are unequal in size, strength, and intelligence. Yet it declared that members of the human race who are unequal in all these respects are created equal in their fundamental rights, beginning with the right to life. Tragically, this principle of equal human rights for all has not always been followed in practice, even by the Declaration's signers. But in our nation's proudest moments Americans have realized that we cannot dismiss or exclude any class of humanity—that basic human rights must belong to all members of the human race without distinction. In light of modern knowledge about the continuity of human development from conception onwards, all of us—without regard to religious affiliation—confront this challenge again today when we make decisions about human beings at the embryonic stage of development.

Finally, some claim that scientists who kill embryos for their stem cells are not actually depriving anyone of life, because they are using "spare" or unwanted embryos who will die anyway. This argument is simply invalid. Ultimately each of us will die, but that gives no one a right to kill us. Our society does not permit lethal experiments on terminally ill patients or condemned prisoners on the pretext that they will soon die anyway. Likewise, the fact that an embryonic human being is at risk of being abandoned by his or her parents gives no individual or government a right to directly kill that human being first. . . .

Stem Cell Research Is Unethical

The issue of stem cell research does not force us to choose between science and ethics, much less between science and religion. It presents a choice as to *how* our society will pursue scientific and medical progress. Will we ignore ethical norms and use some of the most vulnerable human beings as objects, undermining the respect for human life that is at the foundation of the healing arts? Such a course, even if it led to rapid technical progress, would be a regress in our efforts to build a society that is fully human. Instead we must pursue progress in ethically responsible ways that respect the dignity of each human being. Only this will produce cures and treatments that everyone can live with.

Analyze the essay:

1. In the previous essay Michael J. Sandel argued it is ethical to use spare embryos from fertility treatments in stem cell research because they are going to be discarded anyway. How do the authors of this essay respond to this argument? After reading both essays, with whom do you agree?

2. The authors of this viewpoint grounded their arguments in religious beliefs. Briefly describe the ways in which religion was used to argue against stem cell research. Then, state your opinion on the matter. Do you think it is possible to be religious and also support stem cell research? Or do you agree with the authors and believe that God would consider the destruction of embryos to be murder? Explain your reasoning.

Adult Stem Cells Can Cure Disease Better than Embryonic Stem Cells

Chris Banescu

In the following essay Chris Banescu argues that adult stem cells can cure disease better than embryonic stem cells. Although it has been touted as a miracle cure, Banescu says that embryonic stem cell research has yet to successfully treat or cure a single disease. But research using adult stem cells has successfully produced treatment for cancer, eye, heart, and blood diseases, and many other disorders. Banescu concludes that since it has not been proved to be effective and has significant ethical issues, funding embryonic stem cell research is waste of time and money. He says because it is unproved and fraught with moral problems, politicians should stop endorsing embryonic stem cell research and support the development of adult stem cell research instead.

Banescu is an attorney, entrepreneur, author, speaker, and professor.

Consider the following questions:

1. What significance does the term "embryonic human beings" have in the context of the viewpoint?
2. What did an April 2007 report find about the curative potential of adult stem cells, according to Banescu?
3. Who is Dr. Arnold Kriegstein, and how does he factor into the author's argument?

Chris Banescu, "Obama: Destroying Human Life for the 'Greater Good,'" ChrisBanescu.com, March 17, 2009. Reproduced by permission.

On March 9th [2009] President [Barack] Obama's executive order reversed the [former president George W.] Bush administration's long-standing restrictions on using federal funds for embryonic stem cells research and authorized the destruction of live human embryos in medical experimentation. The administration ignored the promising results from adult stem cell therapies. It reopened a Pandora's box of bioethical concerns and raised vocal opposition from many Christian leaders, including 191 Catholic bishops.

Science is on the side of embryonic stem cell research, the president argued. Linking fetal stem cells experiments with "scientific integrity" in the order titled "Signing of Stem Cell Executive Order and Scientific Integrity," Obama proclaimed:

> we will lift the ban on federal funding for promising embryonic stem cell research. We will vigorously support scientists who pursue this research. And we will aim for America to lead the world in the discoveries it one day may yield.

But is the grandiose promise and lofty language supported by the facts?

Adult vs. Embryonic Stem Cells

Stem cell research focuses on both adult (somatic) [or body] stem cells and embryonic stem cells. Adult stem cells are undifferentiated cells, found inside the tissues and organs of the body, that are capable of regenerating damaged tissue or self-renewing indefinitely. Under the right conditions, these cells have the potential to transform themselves into any other cell type.

Embryonic stem cells, as the name suggests, are derived from embryos. This process requires the harvesting and destruction of live human embryos that have been fertilized in vitro and then destroyed at the blastocyst stage, about four to five days into development.

Experimentation using adult stem cells raises no moral issues since no embryo is destroyed. Embryonic stem cells research on the other hand, requires the creation and destruction of living embryos and is fraught with moral difficulty. That's why almost half of all Americans oppose it, many scientists and doctors have gone on the record to express their deep misgivings about the procedure, and why religious leaders condemn it.

Strong Opposition by Christian Churches

The Catholic Church (1.1 billion members world-wide), the Baptist churches (38 million believers), and the Orthodox Church (225 million faithful) condemn all forms of embryonic stem cell research.

In June of 2008, the US Conference of Catholic Bishops (USCCB), in a statement devoted exclusively to the issue of embryonic stem cell research, reiterated the Church's long-standing belief that human life is a precious gift from God and deserves protection and the greatest respect. The hierarchs condemned the direct killing of innocent "embryonic human beings" in the interest of research and opposed the use of taxpayer funds to support such policies. The USCCB statement made it very clear that harvesting embryonic cells is a deliberate act that kills human life, a "gravely immoral act."

In October 2001, the Synod of Bishops of the Orthodox Church in America (OCA), in a statement titled "Embryonic Stem Cell Research in the Perspective of Orthodox Christianity," also affirmed the sanctity of all human life, created in the image of God, which begins at the moment of conception. The Orthodox bishops

The Curative Power of Adult Stem Cells

Adult stem cells, which occur in small quantities in organs throughout the body for natural growth and repair, have become stars despite great skepticism early on. Though this is a more difficult task, scientists have learned to coax them to mature into many cell types, like brain and heart cells, in the laboratory. (Such stem cells can be removed almost as easily as drawing a unit of blood, and they have been used successfully for years in bone marrow transplants.) To date, most of the stem cell triumphs that the public hears about involve the infusion of adult stem cells. We've just recently seen separate research reports of patients with spinal cord injury and multiple sclerosis benefiting from adult stem cell therapy.

Bernadine Healy, "Why Embryonic Stem Cells Are Obsolete," *USA Today*, March 4, 2009.

Adult Stem Cell Therapies Treat Many Diseases

Supporters of adult stem cell research claim human patients suffering from many diseases have seen results from therapies based on adult stem cells, whereas embryonic stem cell research has yet to cure a single disease.

Cancers

1. Brain Cancer
2. Retinoblastoma
3. Ovarian Cancer
4. Skin Cancer: Merkel Cell Carcinoma
5. Testicular Cancer
6. Tumors Abdominal Organs Lymphoma
7. Non-Hodgkin's Lymphoma
8. Hodgkin's Lymphoma
9. Acute Lymphoblastic Leukemia
10. Acute Myelogenous Leukemia
11. Chronic Myelogenous Leukemia
12. Juvenile Myelomonocytic Leukemia
13. Chronic Myelomonocytic Leukemia
14. Cancer of the Lymph Nodes: Angioimmunoblastic Lymphadenopathy
15. Multiple Myeloma
16. Myelodysplasia
17. Breast Cancer
18. Neuroblastoma
19. Renal Cell Carcinoma
20. Soft Tissue Sarcoma
21. Various Solid Tumors
22. Ewing's Sarcoma
23. Waldenstrom's Macroglobulinemia
24. Hemophagocytic Lymphohistiocytosis
25. Poems Syndrome
26. Myelofibrosis

Autoimmune Diseases

27. Diabetes Type I (Juvenile)
28. Systemic Lupus
29. Sjogren's Syndrome
30. Myasthenia
31. Autoimmune Cytopenia
32. Scleromyxedema
33. Scleroderma
34. Crohn's Disease
35. Behcet's Disease
36. Rheumatoid Arthritis
37. Juvenile Arthritis
38. Multiple Sclerosis
39. Polychondritis
40. Systemic Vasculitis
41. Alopecia Universalis
42. Buerger's Disease

Cardiovascular

43. Acute Heart Damage
44. Chronic Coronary Artery Disease

Ocular

45. Corneal Regeneration

Immunodeficiencies

46. Severe Combined Immunodeficiency Syndrome
47. X-Linked Lymphoproliferative Syndrome
48. X-Linked Hyper Immunoglobulin M Syndrome

Neural Degenerative Diseases & Injuries

49. Parkinson's Disease
50. Spinal Cord Injury
51. Stroke Damage

Anemias & Other Blood Conditions

52. Sickle Cell Anemia
53. Sideroblastic Anemia
54. Aplastic Anemia
55. Red Cell Aplasia
56. Amegakaryocytic Thrombocytopenia
57. Thalassemia
58. Primary Amyloidosis
59. Diamond Blackfan Anemia
60. Fanconi's Anemia
61. Chronic Epstein-Barr Infection

Wounds And Injuries

62. Limb Gangrene
63. Surface Wound Healing
64. Jawbone Replacement
65. Skull Bone Repair

Other Metabolic Disorders

66. Hurler's Syndrome
67. Osteogenesis Imperfecta
68. Krabbe Leukodystrophy
69. Osteopetrosis
70. Cerebral X-Linked Adrenoleukodystrophy

Liver Disease

71. Chronic Liver Failure
72. Liver Cirrhosis

Bladder Disease

73. End-Stage Bladder Disease

Taken from: The Coalition of Americans for Research Ethics, April 11, 2007.

denounced any research based on the destruction of embryonic cells, regardless of its potential benefits. The Church's position is clear that a live embryo is human life and not just a "clump of cells." Destroying them to extract stem cells for research purposes is "morally and ethically wrong in every instance."

Richard Land, president of the Southern Baptist Ethics & Religious Liberty Commission (ERLC), also denounced Obama's decision as a "sad day for the sanctity of all human life in America." Mr. Land labeled the president's action "open season on unborn babies" for endorsing the destruction of human life for the purpose of harvesting of cells and tissues in the interests of science.

From a moral standpoint, adult stem cells clearly provide the least controversial solution. But what about the science? Which approach has shown the most promise and provided the better medical results?

Medical Success from Adult Stem Cells

In 2007, the Coalition of Americans for Research Ethics compiled and published a paper showing the impressive success of adult stem cell therapies. Titled "Peer-Reviewed References List Showing Applications of Adult Stem Cells That Produce Therapeutic Benefit to Human Patients," the report documented over 70 treatments and 1,300 human clinical trials for adult stem cells research.

As of April 2007, adult stem cells research had produced treatments for approximately 26 types of cancers, 19 auto-immune diseases, 2 cardiovascular and 1 ocular problems, 3 immunodeficiencies, 3 neural degenerative diseases and injuries, 10 anemias and other blood conditions, 4 wounds and injuries, 5 different metabolic disorders, 2 types of liver disease, and 1 bladder disease. On the other hand, no embryonic stem cells research had made it past the animal testing phase.

A summary score card of these findings [is] adult stem cells = 70, embryonic stem cells = 0.

A brief overview of the available studies and articles published since April 2007 point to continuing successes and advances in the field. . . .

Adult Stem Cells Are Worth Investing In

The suitability of adult stem cells for potential cures and the many medical successes have attracted significant financial support from private companies, universities, and venture capitalists. The same cannot be said about embryonic stem cells experimentation. This is due to the lack of any medical evidence where a malady has been healed using embryonic stem cells, the difficult ethical and moral issues raised, and the tendency of these treatments to produce tumors as a side effect, including the recent discovery of brain and spinal cord tumors in a young man in Israel undergoing fetal stem cell therapy.

The lack of private capital is the reason embryonic stem cell advocates are beating down the doors of government. In his criticism of California's Proposition 71 (which authorized $3 billion of state funds to support embryonic experimentation), social ethicist Wesley J. Smith explained:

> Think about it. If this were really likely to bring about cures any time soon, you would have to beat venture capitalists away with a stick. But the money to pay for cloning and embryonic stem cell research is not flowing from the private sector, so they want the public to pay for the research with borrowed money that is not accountable to the legislature.

The Facts Are Against Embryonic Stem Cell Research

Obama's support of embryonic stem cell research is ideologically driven. The facts don't support his promises or claims of scientific integrity. By lifting the federal ban he endorses highly speculative and unproven experimentation, using taxpayer dollars to fund it. His words ring with pseudo-religious fervor.

Even Nicholas Wade, writing in the *New York Times*, hinted that Obama's adamant endorsement of embryonic stem cells experimentation is misguided. In a March 10, 2009 article titled "Rethink Stem Cells? Science Already Has" the *NYT* questioned the need for embryonic research when better advances have been made using adult cells that can be "reprogrammed to an embryonic state with surprising ease." According to [University of California at San Francisco stem cell researcher] Dr. [Arnold] Kriegstein the advances made by biologist Shinya Yamanaka from Japan in reprogramming these cells may "eventually eclipse the embryonic stem cell lines for therapeutic as well as diagnostics applications."

In a surprising twist from the left-leaning paper, it also admitted that:

> Despite an F.D.A.-approved safety test of embryonic stem cells in spinal cord injury that the Geron Corporation began in January, many scientists believe that putting stem-cell-derived tissues into patients lies a long way off. Embryonic stem cells have their drawbacks. They cause tumors, and the adult cells derived from them may be rejected by the patient's immune system. Furthermore, whatever disease process caused the patients' tissue cells to die is likely to kill introduced cells as well. All these problems may be solvable, but so far none have been solved.

We Must Protect Life

Coming on the heels of the promise last month to overturn the "conscience clause" that prevents pro-life hospitals and doctors from being forced to perform abortions,

Obama's lifting of the ban on federal funds for embryonic stem cell research is a troubling sign. Protecting life in its earliest stages and ignoring those who seek to protect it, takes a back seat to the designs of social utilitarians in this new administration. We've heard the promises before, some from leaders we would rather forget.

Analyze the essay:

1. Chris Banescu quotes from several sources to support the points he makes in his essay. Make a list of everyone he quotes, including their credentials and the nature of their comments. Then, analyze his sources—are they credible? Are they well qualified to speak on this subject? What specific points do they support?

2. Banescu says one reason adult stem cells seem more likely to cure disease better than embryonic stem cells is because private companies, universities, and individuals have primarily invested in adult stem cell research, whereas the government is the primary investor in embryonic stem cell research. Explain what he means. Then, state whether you agree—do you think that who invests in a technology is a good indicator of its value? Why or why not?

Adult Stem Cells Are Not as Curative as Embryonic Stem Cells

Coalition for the Advancement of Medical Research

The Coalition for the Advancement of Medical Research is a bipartisan coalition composed of one hundred nationally recognized patient organizations, universities, scientific societies, and foundations. In the following essay they argue that embryonic stem cell research is probably more promising than research using adult stem cells, but both should be funded for science's sake. Although embryonic stem cell research is controversial, they explain it has enormous curative potential. In fact, the authors say, it was embryonic stem cell research that allowed researchers to discover how to use adult stem cells in the first place. They claim that adult stem cell research has only had narrow success, and it would be a mistake for the investors and the government to focus solely on that path of research. They remind readers to be patient, as important medical breakthroughs often take decades to be achieved. They conclude that embryonic stem cell research has enormous value and promise and should not be abandoned in favor of adult stem cell research.

A Catalyst for Cures: Embryonic Stem Cell Research. Washington, DC.: Coalition for the Advancement of Medical Research, 2009. Reprinted with the permission of the Coalition for the Advancement of Medical Research.

Human embryonic stem cell (hESC) research has reached a 10-year milestone. In 1998, James Thomson and John Gearhart separately announced they had successfully grown the first human pluripotent [that is, has multiple uses] stem cell lines in culture, cells that can self-renew and give rise to various cell types in the body. Despite limited funding, scientists have made great strides in using these primary cells to understand what goes wrong in disease and begin to devise promising new therapies for devastating conditions, such as heart disease, spinal cord injury, and diabetes. Conversations with some of the nation's top stem cell researchers—in academia and industry—make clear that, with removal of limits on Federal funding, hESC research will fulfill its promise in broader ways than originally anticipated.

It is time for the government to become a full scientific partner in supporting the broad range of stem cell research so that the greatest public benefit can be achieved on the shoulders of the last 10 years' accomplishments.

Embryonic Stem Cell Research Has Achieved a Lot

In 1998, researchers imagined that hES cells could be made into any kind of cell in the body. Ten years ago, this was a hope. Today it is fact. Researchers have shown that stem cells from embryos have the ability to become many of the roughly 210 cell types in the human body. They have coaxed hES cells to form heart cells, dopamine-producing brain cells, motor neurons, bladder tissue, kidney tissue, and others.

Two out of three major, early goals for hES cells have been met:

1. hES cells would be a vehicle for learning about tissue development and about the relationship of tissues and genes. They would lead to the discovery of the genes involved in self-renewal. Those promises have been realized.
2. hES cells would offer a path to new treatments. Now that scientists know how to make heart muscle and dopamine-producing cells, for example, the goals of cell therapies have moved from the theoretical to the concrete. hESC-derived cells are beginning to be used for early toxicity screening and new drug discovery, as well.
3. There would be widespread use and testing of these cells. Restrictive Federal policies severely diminished that expectation.

"Everything we expected hES cells to do, they are doing," says James Thomson, University of Wisconsin. "They've proven themselves."

Stem Cell Research Is More Promising Today than It Was Ten Years Ago

"In the next decade, most advances will come from drugs that affect progression of disease. And we'll get there by using hES cells as test beds for new therapeutics," says Doug Melton, Harvard Stem Cell Institute.

After 10 years of experience with hES cells, scientists know what needs to be done to make ES-based cells useful for patients—and the opportunities go far beyond cell transplantation.

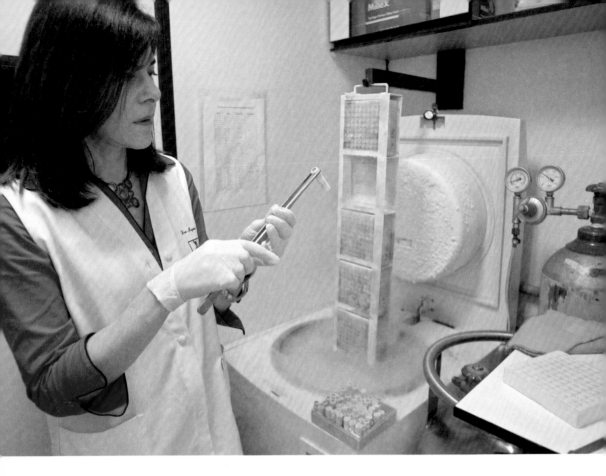

Research with all types of stem cells must continue in order to discover new treatments and therapies.

The scientific community is asking questions it would not have asked if it didn't have access to hES cells. And hES cell studies led to the unexpected development of induced pluripotent stem (iPS) cells, adult cells that are reprogrammed to an embryonic stem cell-like state by being forced to express factors important for maintaining pluripotency. Now we even have proof that you can take a fully mature cell and put genes into it and drive it in a different direction. Pancreatic exocrine cells, for example, can be transformed to pancreatic beta cells, the cells that are destroyed in type 1 diabetes. All of these advances are a result of hES cell research. . . .

hES cells are an unbeatable research tool to understand the body and what goes wrong in disease. Just like telescopes opened new vistas to distant galaxies, hES cells offer unprecedented access to the human body. Scientists are using hES cells to grow limitless quantities of various tissues, such as heart muscle cells. It will be a vast improvement over today's studies of the physiology of the human heart, which rely on limited biopsy samples from sick hearts.

We Cannot Allow Embryonic Stem Cell Research to Wither

Some opposed to hESC research have argued that we don't need hES cells anymore, now that iPS cells have been developed. But if we have learned anything in the history of stem cell research, it is that we have not been very good at predicting which cells are most useful for which applications. To devise new therapies, research must continue with all types of stem cells. If we allow research on hES cells to wither, who knows how many other breakthroughs, like adult cell reprogramming, will go undiscovered. Although iPS cells show great promise, preliminary studies indicate they are not identical to hES cells and may not be as useful for some applications. And there appears to be significant variation between iPS cell lines, probably more so than between human ES cell lines. Further studies are necessary. In terms of safety, iPS cells are much further from the clinic than are ES cells. At present, they are made with genes and viruses that can cause cancer.

> ### No Good Replacement for Embryonic Stem Cells
>
> Adult stem cells could not be used to produce cellular models of human disease as cloning and the production of embryonic stem cell lines could. . . . Work over the past two years has convincingly demonstrated that adult stem cells will not replace ES [embryonic stem] cells. Both cell types are different; they both have their advantages and disadvantages and will be useful for particular purposes. In some cases, combined ES cell and adult stem cell therapy might be the best option.
>
> Katrien Devolder and Julian Savulescu, "A Defense of Stem Cell and Cloning Research," Oxford Uehiro Centre for Practical Ethics, 2006. www.practical ethics.ox.ac.uk/Pubs/Savulescu/stemcellresearch.pdf.

"We are doing very careful comparisons of how well iPS cells and hES cells make motor neurons, and how functional those cells truly are," says Kevin Eggan, Harvard University. "NIH [the National Institutes of Health] should be funding both activities."

Every study of iPS cells requires hES cells for controls and comparisons. These comparisons are crucial for moving the iPS field forward. Researchers must test the safety and efficacy of iPS cells against hES cells. Continued research on hES cells and others may reveal other ways to accomplish regenerative medicine. But we are not there yet. . . .

Adult Stem Cells Have Had Only Narrow Success

Many scientists have been studying adult stem cells and learning more about their utility and their limitations. So far, adult stem cells have only successfully been used in a very narrow area: blood system reconstitution, including bone marrow transplant, umbilical cord transplant, and peripheral blood transplant.

"If you're a botanist, you don't study one type of tree to learn everything about trees," says Ole Isacson, Harvard Medical School.

Human embryos (pictured) provide embryonic stem cells, which the viewpoint asserts are an unmatched tool for understanding what goes wrong with the body during disease.

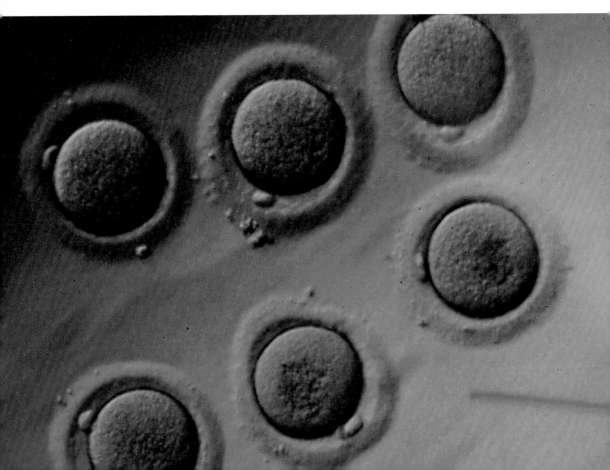

The Majority of Americans Want the Government to Fund Stem Cell Research

A 2009 Gallup poll found that the majority of Americans —52 percent—support either easing restrictions or placing no restrictions on government funding of stem cell research.

Question: "Which would you prefer the government to do: place no restrictions on government funding of stem cell research, ease the current restrictions to allow more stem cell research, keep the current restrictions in place, or should the government not fund stem cell research at all?"

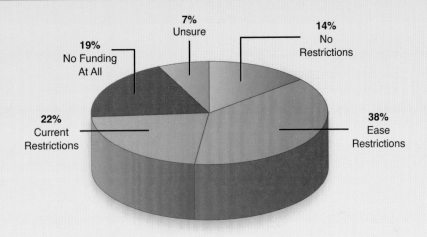

7%
Unsure

14%
No
Restrictions

19%
No Funding
At All

22%
Current
Restrictions

38%
Ease
Restrictions

Taken from: Gallup poll, February 20–22, 2009.

In 2006, [Japanese scientist Shinya] Yamanaka first reported he had turned mouse adult skin cells into stem cells. Then late in 2007, Yamanaka, Thomson, and [George] Daley each reported that they had successfully turned human adult skin cells into stem cells. The development of these iPS cells was unexpected. The prevailing wisdom was that, once a cell had become differentiated or specialized, it could not be turned back by any method other than nuclear transfer. But that's just what iPS does. iPS cells are a victory for ES cells. They demonstrate the power of stem cell science to lead to unexpected and field-changing breakthroughs. . . .

The Research Is Just Beginning

"It's like discovering nuclear power . . . and now we have to figure out how to use it," says Ole Isacson. His group discovered they could make dopamine-producing cells from hES cells in 2002. But it took much more work to learn how to modify the factors that control the process, and how to do it consistently and with high efficiency. Research takes time. A few examples from history:

- The poliovirus was first isolated in 1909. It took 45 years to get to the Salk vaccine.
- HIV [the virus that causes AIDS] was first isolated in 1983. Bringing all the power of modern virology—and billions of dollars to bear—hundreds of scientists are still working on combating this virus.
- The first attempt at bone marrow transplantation between an unrelated donor and recipient was in 1955 by E. Donnall Thomas—after many years of research. All six patients died. He went back to the lab to figure out why. The first successful transplant of these adult stem cells occurred in 1969—14 years later. It took years more of clinical testing to get it right, and bone marrow transplantation only became a common procedure in the 1980s. If opponents, after 10 years of study of these adult stem cells, had said "there've been no cures, let's stop," then adult cell transplantation would not exist and countless lives would not have been saved.

Scientists need the time and support to overcome safety concerns for using ES cells in patients. There won't be products for patients unless scientists can devise ways to eliminate risk. Parkinson's researcher Ole Isacson is sorting stem-cell derived neural cells to remove those that have tumor-causing potential. This isn't headline-grabbing, but it's critical science.

Analyze the essay:

1. The authors of this essay consider adult stem cell research to be an outgrowth of embryonic stem cell research and therefore argue that success with adult stem cells is only proof of how important it is to continue embryonic stem cell research. How do you think Chris Banescu, author of the previous viewpoint, would respond to this argument?

2. In this essay the authors suggest the best thing scientists can do is focus their energy on both embryonic *and* adult stem cell research in the hope of allowing as much scientific discovery as possible. What is your opinion of this suggestion? Write two or three sentences on whether you consider this suggestion to be realistic, impossible, good advice, poor planning, or something else.

Stem Cell Research Will Lead to the Cloning of Humans

William L. Saunders Jr., David Prentice, and Michael A. Fragoso

In the following essay William L. Saunders Jr., David Prentice, and Michael A. Fragoso warn that stem cell research involves human cloning and should thus be rejected. They explain that the process by which research embryos are created—somatic cell nuclear transfer (SCNT)—is a form of human cloning. Some people do not consider SCNT to be cloning because the cloned embryos are created in a petri dish and destroyed when they are harvested for stem cells just a few days after their creation. But Saunders, Prentice, and Fragoso argue that the purpose for which something is cloned does not matter—the fact is, they say, embryos created in a petri dish for stem cell research have been cloned and would develop into people if inserted into a host human and allowed to gestate. They therefore oppose embryonic stem cell research on the grounds that it involves human cloning, which they consider immoral.

Saunders, Prentice, and Fragoso all work for the Family Research Council, a pro-life Christian organization and think tank dedicated to preserving the sanctity of human life, traditional marriage, and other conservative issues.

Consider the following questions:

1. What, according to the authors, does Dolly the sheep have in common with embryos used in stem cell research?
2. Who is Larry Goldstein and on what grounds do the authors disagree with his view of stem cell research?
3. Why do the authors consider it a "linguistic trick" to describe embryos as "microscopic dividing cells in a Petri dish"?

In recent years, a growing number of state governments have embarked on cloning initiatives, often linked to efforts to promote human embryonic stem cell research. Legislation has ranged from protecting certain kinds of human cloning and embryonic stem cell research (i.e., ensuring they cannot be "outlawed"), to funding the practices directly. One can only expect that, given the inflated media coverage, this trend will continue.

State Measures to Fund Cloning

The best known of these initiatives were in California and Missouri. Each amended the state constitution, rather than state laws, making repeal more difficult. California's Proposition 71 from 2004, known as the "California Stem Cell Research and Cures Initiative" ("Prop 71"), was crafted specifically to fund embryonic stem cell research and human cloning, while the 2006 Missouri Amendment 2, "The Missouri Stem Cell Research and Cures Initiative" ("Amendment 2"), enshrined the right to engage in human cloning in the Missouri state constitution.

Supporters of both measures made similar claims—that embryonic stem cell research and human cloning provide effective cures for diseases; that embryonic stem cell research and cloning would provide economic growth; and that by enshrining embryonic stem cell research and cloning in law, the state would provide meaningful ethical oversight.

Yet each one of these claims is false. . . .

Cloning Is Cloning Is Cloning

SCNT is the process by which someone or something is cloned. It is the same procedure that gave us Dolly the Sheep. It really is the definition of cloning, i.e. removing the nucleus of an "egg" (or, oocyte) and replacing it with the nucleus from an ordinary body (or "somatic") cell; this is *somatic cell nuclear transfer* or SCNT.

The proponents of Amendment 2 played a semantic game, changing the definition of cloning from the creation of a genetically identical human being to the creation (and *implantation*) of a genetically identical human being *for reproductive purposes*. Thus the Missouri "cloning *ban*" does no such thing; it merely bans a specific *motivation* for cloning. If you want to create it to kill it, that's okay. If you want to create it to bring it to birth, that isn't. As one newspaper put it following the passage of this deceptive initiative, "a clone by any other name, such as 'somatic cell nuclear transfer,' is still a clone."

Stem Cell Research Involves Newly Created Life

The proponents, however, could not disagree more. William Neaves, President and CEO of the Stowers Institute for Medical Research, insists to this day that, "It does not represent a newly conceived life. It has been cultured in a lab dish from an ordinary body cell of an already-living person conceived years ago." This statement is a mixture of technical truths that actually implies a falsehood. A cloned embryo is not, in fact, "conceived" as conception is normally understood, that is, as involving normal, sexual reproduction. It *is* created, in a "lab dish" from a "body cell," in a sense, as noted above. But none of this is germane to what *it* is: namely a new, living *human being*.

Neaves has made such declarations in the past. "When people hear the phrase 'clone a human being' they think of an attempt to make a human version of Dolly the sheep. No one thinks of making a few dozen cells in a Petri dish," Neaves told the *Washington Post*. However, if people think that the sort of cloning Neaves advocates is "an attempt to make a human version of Dolly the sheep," they are absolutely *right*. Dolly the sheep was created *by the same process of SCNT* that was legalized in Missouri. Dolly the sheep was at first a *sheep* embryo *just as the embryos* Neaves wants to use for stem cell research are *human* embryos.

Some believe that embryonic stem cell research will encourage women to sell their eggs for research, an act that a 2006 Missouri proposal sought to ban.

People who make the scientific argument that embryos are embryos regardless of how they were made, and thus cloning is cloning, whatever the purpose, are written off by Neaves as religious fundamentalists. He says that basing public policy on the facts of cloning "would be comparable to outlawing blood transfusions because some Christians believe it's wrong." Scientific observations with which he disagrees become "beliefs."

Life Is Killed When Embryos Are Destroyed

Neaves' California counterpart, Larry Goldstein, once said of pro-lifers, "Another downside is that some opponents of embryonic stem cell research speak about this research in terms of Nazi-type experiments, or violating the civil rights of embryos, or murdering blastocysts. They often make outrageous and totally distorted scientific claims because they don't actually understand the science. I feel bad about the implications that I'm a murderer when I'm driven actually trying to do something good and trying to educate the public. It's difficult when opponents feel no compunction about scientific distortions and falsehoods." However, Goldstein's statements merely confuse the issues.

That embryo-destructive research kills blastocysts (which are humans in a predictable stage of embryonic development) is indisputable scientifically. Whether blastocysts are "murdered" in "Nazi-type experiments" or embryos "have their civil rights violated" is a *philosophical* question about the dignity and inviolability of innocent human life, on which proponents and opponents of human cloning disagree. Yet Goldstein describes this *moral* disagreement as "outrageous and

Cloning to Kill

With no federal ban on cloning, some states have provided funding for it under the guise of a "ban," setting up the distinction between reproductive cloning (creating an embryo to ultimately raise as a child) and research or therapeutic cloning (creating an embryo to use for medical purposes). In the end, though, the process is the same; in therapeutic cloning, you are cloning to kill.

Kathryn Lopez, "Cloning by Any Other Name Is Still Cloning," *Jewish World Review*, June 12, 2007. www.jewishworldreview.com/0607/lopez061207.php3.

totally distorted *scientific* claims" (Emphasis added). However, the science is indisputable—embryo-destruction kills blastocysts. Goldstein confuses his categories by referring to the *moral consequences* of the science *as the science itself*. Goldstein dismisses his opponent's science as mere ideology, while Neaves simply dismisses his opponents themselves as religious fundamentalists. . . .

All Forms of Cloning Must Be Banned

If a state really wants to ban cloning, it must ban the intentional creation of genetically identical human beings at any stage—regardless of purpose. In fact, a grassroots organization in Missouri, Cures without Cloning, is trying to do just that in the wake of Amendment 2. In their own ballot initiative, seeking to amend the Missouri constitution, Cures without Cloning proposes defining cloning by saying,

> For all purposes within this article, "Clone or attempt to clone a human being" means create or attempt to create a human embryo at any stage, which shall include the one-cell stage onward, by any means other than fertilization of a human egg by a human sperm.

This definition attempts to ban the *act* of cloning, unlike the current law which simply bans a motivation for doing so.

Nevertheless, Cures without Cloning faced more of the same semantic distortions from the pro-cloning forces in Missouri. On October 11, 2007, Robin Carnahan, Missouri's Secretary of State, issued the official ballot summary for the anti-cloning initiative saying that it seeks "to repeal the current ban on human cloning or attempted cloning and to limit Missouri patients' access to stem cell research, therapies and cures approved by voters in November 2006." In other words, expanding a

Dolly the sheep (pictured) was created using a technique called somatic cell nuclear transfer (SCNT), the same process used in embryonic stem cell research.

partial cloning ban to cover *all* cloning is, according to her, a *repeal* of a cloning ban. By Carnahan's logic more is less and less is more.

The *St. Louis Post-Dispatch* said, in defense of Carnahan, that pro-life activists want to prohibit stem cell research and preserve "microscopic dividing cells in a Petri dish." This, as we have shown above, simply dehumanizes the embryo by a linguistic trick.

In response to this double-talk from both Carnahan and the media, a lawsuit was brought by Cures without Cloning alleging bias in the ballot summary. On February 20, Cole County Circuit Judge Patricia Joyce ruled that the existing ballot language was "insufficient and unfair." The description was changed to say the purpose of the initiative is "prohibiting human cloning that is conducted by creating a human embryo at any stage from the one-cell stage forward; prohibiting expenditure of taxpayer dollars on research or experimentation on human cloning; and allowing stem cell research for therapies and cures that complies with these prohibitions and the prohibitions of Section 38(d) of the Constitution."

Regrettably, the state court of appeals overturned this decision, changing the language to read that the initiative would "change the current ban"—rather than Carnahan's preferred "repeal the current ban." The decision came so late in the political process that it prevented Missouri pro-life groups from putting the initiative on the November 2008 ballot, which is precisely what the pro-cloners wanted.

Be Wary of Future Attempts to Legalize Cloning

In the future many states will be tempted to pass constitutional amendments similar to California's Prop 71 and Missouri's Amendment 2. They will be attracted to human cloning and embryonic stem cell research by the same siren songs of miracle cures, expanded revenue, and ethical benchmarks. As we have seen, all of these claims are overstated. The cures are not forthcoming. The revenue is purely hypothetical. The ethics are mere doublespeak.

Analyze the essay:

1. Saunders, Prentice, and Fragoso think it is immoral to clone embryos for the sake of science, even though these embryos comprise just a few cells in a petri dish that live for about a week. What is your view of these embryos? Do you view them as potential humans who have a right to live? Or do you think the potentially life-saving research conducted on them is more valuable? Explain your position and support your ideas with quotes from the texts you have read.

2. The authors of this essay reject embryonic stem cell research because they believe that life begins at conception—thus, they believe embryos used in research are potential persons who have a right to life. What is your opinion on when life begins? What bearing does that have on your view of stem cell research?

Stem Cell Research Will Not Lead to the Cloning of Humans or Other Atrocities

Marty Kaplan

In the following essay Marty Kaplan argues that stem cell research will not result in the cloning of humans, euthanizing the disabled, stealing organs from sick people, or any other nightmare scenario. He disagrees with those who warn that supporting embryonic stem cell research will result in these awful situations. Kaplan says human beings are refined, complex beings capable of making distinctions and exceptions—there is no need to think that just because they embrace one type of powerful technology that has scientific good (such as using embryonic stem cell research to cure disease) it will automatically result in immoral applications of that technology (such as cloning armies of humans or making man-animal hybrids). Kaplan says it is irrational to fear that scientists will use stem cell research to such ends, and he thinks the unlikely possibility of such scenarios is no reason to reject such important technology.

Kaplan is a professor of entertainment, media, and society at the USC Annenberg School for Communication.

Consider the following questions:

1. What is "slippery slope" reasoning as it pertains to stem cell research, and why does Kaplan disagree with it?
2. What are cowumans and humabbits, and how do they factor into Kaplan's argument?
3. What does the term "federal anvils" mean in the context of the essay?

O f all the arguments against stem cell research, the lamest has to be that "it would put us on a slippery slope." But since this case comes from the same precincts that gave us "gay marriage will lead to incest and man-on-dog sex," I suppose I shouldn't be surprised.

We Need Not Fear a Slippery Slope

The anti-stem-cell slippery slope argument goes like this: If you permit scientists to destroy human embryos for the purpose of research, it's a slippery slope from there to killing human fetuses in order to harvest tissue, and from there to euthanizing disabled or terminally ill people to harvest their organs, and from there to human cloning and human-animal hybrids, and if making chimeras is OK, well then Dr. Frankenstein must also be OK, and Dr. [Josef] Mengele [a Nazi doctor who conducted unethical experiments on people], too, and before you know it, it's one long hapless inevitable slide from high-minded medicine to the Nazis.

This is not the same as the argument over when human life begins. If the answer to that is, when a sperm cell fertilizes an egg, then a single-cell zygote is already a tiny human being with a soul, and anything that stops it from becoming a fully-developed person is evil and must be outlawed. This way of thinking leads not only to ruling out exceptions for abortion in cases of rape, incest, a fatal genetic disorder or a threat to the mother's health; it also means a ban on in vitro fertilization, because that technique also leads to the destruction of superfluous embryos, unless of course you're the octo-mom [referring to Nadya Suleman, who gave birth to octuplets in 2009], but let's not go there just now.

The when-life-begins argument is about logical consistency. Life is life, period, and no compromise, even for the most compassionate of reasons, is possible. How then do its adherents justify, say, killing

people in self-defense, or in war? The answer is that those circumstances are sanctioned by the Bible, every word of which was divinely written. If that's fundamentally what you believe, then there's no slippery slope to be concerned about, because you never need to make exceptions to the rules, because all the rules come straight from the Creator.

But the slippery slope argument is all about exceptions. It doesn't require believing that legal rules come from moral rules that in turn come from on high. Instead, it's about what you believe coming from down below, from our innards and our evolutionary forebears. Call it hardwiring, or call it psychology;

The author does not believe stem cell research will lead to a moral slippery slope.

it doesn't matter. What counts is a fundamentalism about human nature.

Humans Are Capable of Making Distinctions

The author argues that stem cell researchers are capable of distinguishing between moral, beneficial research and immoral, unnecessary experimentation.

This view of how people are, deep down, is implicit in the metaphor itself. Picture a person on a steep mountaintop. Then imagine him taking a step off the summit and onto an ice-covered slope. (Please don't be offended that I'm not saying "him or her''; this guy has got to be pretty stupid to take that step.) And following that step comes a cartoonish blur of whirling legs and arms, and before you know it the guy is tumbling

ass over teakettle down the slope, a human snowball banging into trees, helplessly accelerating toward the fatal crevasse below.

What this case against stem cell research is saying is that people are basically animals, slaves to their appetites, incapable of restraining themselves, biologically unequipped to make complex rules, or draw fine distinctions, or debate exceptions, or enforce differences. If we make one exception, and permit a scientist to culture stem cells from discarded human blastocysts, then when that scientist wants to make cowumans and humabbits, society will be totally flummoxed, completely paralyzed, incapable of drawing a legal line and saying no.

If this were actually true, then the message society sends when police don't stop everyone over the speed limit on the freeway is that it must also be OK to be a hit-and-run driver. You know, there's a slippery slope between not arresting someone for smoking a joint and letting drug cartels destroy our cities. If you can restrict the sale of semi-automatic rifles, then you can ban the right to bear arms. If a shoplifter gets off easy, what's to stop a Bernie Madoff from being allowed to walk? If you make hate speech a crime, then it won't be long before free speech is a crime.

> ## Cloning Is Not the Goal
>
> The goal of this process is not to create cloned human beings, but rather to harvest stem cells that can be used to study human development and to treat disease.
>
> U.S. Department of Energy Office of Science, Office of Biological and Environmental Research, Human Genome Project, May 11, 2009. www.ornl.gov/sci/techresources/Human_Genome/elsi/cloning.shtml.

We Need Stem Cell Research for the Greater Good

During George W. Bush's long summer vacation in 2001—the summer when he dismissed the CIA briefer who told him that [Osama] Bin Laden was determined to strike in the United States with "All right, you've covered your ass now"—the big news out of Crawford [Texas, where Bush has a ranch] was his Solomonic decision to permit federally-funded research only on the 78 stem-cell lines already created in privately-funded labs. Those murders, he signaled to his base, had already been committed, so we might as well get some good out of the crimes.

It turns out that only about 20 of those lines were actually usable in laboratories. As a result, over these last 7 1/2 years, when stem-cell researchers might have been racing toward therapies for diseases like juvenile diabetes, cystic fibrosis and muscular dystrophy, they have instead had federal anvils chained to their ankles.

Our Society Should Not Tolerate Extremists

Today, some of those protesting President [Barack] Obama's reversal of President Bush's limits are saying that we don't need any new lines of embryonic stem cells, because recently discovered techniques, like reprogramming human skin cells into iPS—induced pluripotent stem cells—make it unnecessary to depend on embryos. But the potential of iPS is still unclear; at least as promising and worth pursuing are the hundreds of stem cell lines that were created without federal funding during the Bush years, but have not yet benefited from the kind of . . . research that only the National Institutes of Health can support.

If God is dead, [Russian novelist Fyodor] Dostoevsky had Ivan Karamazov say, then anything is possible. This turns out to be exactly wrong. In fact, you can build a just society on the basis of the rule of law, and you can build a good society on the basis of human culture and humanistic values. Despite what [conservative commentator] Bill O'Reilly says, a secular society is not the same as an immoral society. Every American has the right to choose a God to believe in, or not. But no Americans have the right to impose their own theistic absolutes, or their own dark views of human nature, on anyone else. That's what it means to be a pluralistic democratic society. And the last time I looked, being a democracy is not the first step down a slippery slope.

Analyze the essay:

1. Marty Kaplan uses history, facts, logical reasoning, and examples to make his argument that stem cell research will not result in human cloning. He does not, however, use any quotations to support his point. If you were to rewrite this essay and insert quotations, what authorities might you quote from? Where would you place these quotations to bolster the points Kaplan makes?

2. At the heart of Kaplan's argument is the idea that human beings are capable of distinguishing between different situations, and so it is not reasonable to assume they will use a powerful technology like stem cell research for evil ends just because it is technically possible to do so. How might William L. Saunders Jr., David Prentice, and Michael A. Fragoso, authors of the previous essay, respond to this argument? Quote from both texts in your answer. Then, state with which perspective you ultimately agree.

Section Two:
Model Essays
and Writing
Exercises

The Five-Paragraph Essay

An *essay* is a short piece of writing that discusses or analyzes one topic. The five-paragraph essay is a form commonly used in school assignments and tests. Every five-paragraph essay begins with an *introduction*, ends with a *conclusion*, and features three *supporting paragraphs* in the middle.

The Thesis Statement. The introduction includes the essay's thesis statement. The thesis statement presents the argument or point the author is trying to make about the topic. The essays in this book all have different thesis statements because they are making different arguments about stem cell research.

The thesis statement should clearly tell the reader what the essay will be about. A focused thesis statement helps determine what will be in the essay; the subsequent paragraphs are spent developing and supporting its argument.

The Introduction. In addition to presenting the thesis statement, a well-written introductory paragraph captures the attention of the reader and explains why the topic being explored is important. It may provide the reader with background information on the subject matter or feature an anecdote that illustrates a point relevant to the topic. It could also present startling information that clarifies the point of the essay or put forth a contradictory position that the essay will refute. Further techniques for writing an introduction are found later in this section.

The Supporting Paragraphs. The introduction is then followed by three (or more) supporting paragraphs. These are the main body of the essay. Each paragraph presents and develops a *subtopic* that supports the essay's thesis statement. Each subtopic is spearhead-ed by a *topic sentence* and supported by its own facts, details, and examples. The writer can use various kinds of supporting material and details to back up the topic of each supporting paragraph. These may include statistics, quotations from people with special knowledge or expertise, historic facts, and anecdotes. A rule of writing is that specific and concrete examples are more convincing than vague, general, or unsupported assertions.

The Conclusion. The conclusion is the paragraph that closes the essay. Its function is to summarize or reiterate the main idea of the essay. It may recall an idea from the introduction or briefly examine the larger implications of the thesis. Because the conclusion is also the last chance a writer has to make an impression on the reader, it is important that it not simply repeat what has been presented elsewhere in the essay but close it in a clear, final, and memorable way.

Although the order of the essay's component paragraphs is important, they do not have to be written in the order presented here. Some writers like to decide on a thesis and write the introduction paragraph first. Other writers like to focus first on the body of the essay, and write the introduction and conclusion later.

Pitfalls to Avoid

When writing essays about controversial issues such as stem cell research, it is important to remember that disputes over the material are common precisely because there are many different perspectives. Remember to state your arguments in careful and measured terms. Evaluate your topic fairly—avoid overstating negative qualities of one perspective or understating positive qualities of another. Use examples, facts, and details to support any assertions you make.

The Expository Essay

The previous section of this book provided you with samples of writings on stem cell research. All made arguments or advocated a particular position about stem cell research and related topics. All included elements of *expository* writing as well. The purpose of expository writing is to inform the reader about a particular subject. Sometimes a writer will use exposition to simply communicate knowledge; other times, he or she will use exposition to persuade a reader of a particular point of view.

Types of Expository Writing

There are several different types of expository writing. Examples of these types can be found in the viewpoints in the preceding section. The list below provides some ideas on how an exposition could be organized and presented. Each type of writing could be used separately or in combination in five-paragraph essays.

Definition. Definition refers to simply telling what something is. Definitions can be encompassed in a sentence or paragraph. At other times, definitions may take a paragraph or more. The act of defining some topics—especially abstract concepts—can sometimes serve as the focus of entire essays. An example of definition is found in Viewpoint Five by William L. Saunders Jr., David Prentice, and Michael A. Fragoso, who define the process of somatic cell nuclear transfer (SCNT) in order to argue that it constitutes human cloning.

Classification. A classification essay describes and clarifies relationships between things by placing them in different categories, based on their similarities and differences. This can be a good way of organizing and presenting information.

Process. A process essay looks at how something is done. The writer presents events or steps in a chronological or other ordered sequence of steps. Process writing can either inform the reader of a past event or process by which something was made, or instruct the reader on how to do something.

Illustration. Illustration is one of the simplest and most common patterns of expository writing. Simply put, it explains by giving specific and concrete examples. It is an effective technique for making one's writing both more interesting and more intelligible. Michael J. Sandel offers an example of illustration in Viewpoint One. He uses the example of acorns and oak trees to illustrate why embryos are different from fully developed human beings.

Problem/Solution. Problem/solution refers to when the author raises a problem or a question, and then uses the rest of the paragraph or essay to answer the question or provide possible resolutions to the problem. It can be an effective way of drawing in the reader while imparting information to him/her.

Words and Phrases Common to Expository Essays

accordingly	indeed
because	it is important to
consequently	understand
clearly	it makes sense to
first . . . second . . .	it seems as though
third . . .	it then follows that
for example	moreover
for this reason	next
from this	since
perspective	subsequently
furthermore	therefore
evidently	this is why
however	thus

Defining Embryos,
Defining Values

Editor's Notes The following five-paragraph essay uses definition as an organizing principle. A definition essay describes, defines, or clarifies terms, relationships, objects, concepts, positions, or procedures. You can read more about definition essays (and other types of expository essays) in Preface B of this section.

The following essay uses definition to explore two opposing positions on embryonic stem cell research: one that says embryos should be regarded as full-fledged human beings (and thus opposes such research), and another that says embryos are days-old cellular beings that have the potential to become human but are not yet fully human (and thus supports such research). The notes in the margin point out key features of the essay and will help you understand how the essay is organized. Also note that all sources are cited using Modern Language Association (MLA) style.* For more information on how to cite your sources, see Appendix C. In addition, consider the following:

1. How does the introduction engage the reader's attention?
2. What pieces of supporting evidence are used to back up the essay's points and arguments?
3. What purpose do the essay's quotes serve?
4. How does the author transition from one idea to another?
5. How is definition featured in the essay?

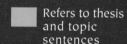
Refers to thesis and topic sentences

Refers to supporting details

Paragraph 1

While embryonic stem cell research has the potential to treat and cure disease, it is controversial because it requires the destruction of an embryo. On first glance one might think it is easy enough to define an embryo, yet arguments over what an embryo is, what rights it should be afforded, and whether it should be regarded as a full human being are precisely what make research involving embryos so controversial. Is an embryo a five-day-old group of rapidly dividing cells? Is it a full-fledged human being that should be offered rights, privileges, and protection? How a person chooses to define an embryo shapes his or her attitude toward embryonic stem cell research.

This is the essay's thesis statement. It tells the reader what the essay will be about.

Paragraph 2

People who oppose embryonic stem cell research define embryos as persons in a pre-infant state. This is because unless it is damaged or naturally miscarried, an embryo will develop into a fetus, and then an infant, and ever forward. "The human embryo, from conception onward, is as much a living member of the human species as any of us," says the United States Conference of Catholic Bishops (USCCB). "Just as each of us was once an adolescent, a child, a newborn infant, and a child in the womb, each of us was once an embryo" (USCCB). Because embryonic stem cell research requires the embryo to be destroyed, the USCCB and other opponents of stem cell research regard the process as nothing less than murder. They believe that all human beings deserve a right to life—no matter what stage of development—and define embryos as full humans waiting to happen.

This is the topic sentence of Paragraph 2. It is a subset of the essay's thesis.

This statement was taken from Viewpoint Two. Learn how to spot quotes that can be used to support your points.

Paragraph 3

In contrast, those who support embryonic stem cell research tend not to define a five-day-old embryo (the stage at which it is destroyed in order to harvest stem cells from it) as a full human being. For them, embryos are a group of cells at the earliest possible stage of development. An embryo does not have a body or any body parts, cannot live on its own, and does not have the ability to hear, think, feel, or see. "It is important to be clear about the embryo from which stem cells are extracted," says Harvard professor Michael J. Sandel. "It is not implanted and growing in a woman's uterus. It is not a fetus. It has

What is the topic sentence of Paragraph 3? How did you recognize it?

This quote was taken from Viewpoint One. What point does it lend support to?

no recognizable human features or form. It is, rather, a blastocyst [a very young embryo], a cluster of 180 to 200 cells, growing in a petri dish, barely visible to the naked eye" (Sandel). In Sandel's opinion, there is more to being human than just the physical potential to grow into one. He compares embryos and persons to acorns and oak trees: cut from the same cloth, yet distinct in essence.

Paragraph 4

The American public is torn between these two definitions of an embryo. On the one hand, Americans agree it is inappropriate to regard embryos as full-scale human beings: This is why, according to the Pew Research Center, the majority of them—56 percent—say it is more important to conduct stem cell research than to avoid destroying embryos used in the research. A 2008 Time magazine poll found similar support for this perspective: 73 percent of Americans say they favor conducting research on embryos discarded after fertility treatment procedures (embryos that were created for the purpose of implanting them into a woman who has difficulty getting pregnant on her own, but for a variety of reasons end up unused). On the other hand, Americans hold a deep respect for embryos and do not take issues involving them lightly. This was evidenced by a Genetics and Public Policy Center poll, which found that 63 percent of Americans attribute a high moral status to embryos, meaning they consider them to have the same rights as humans and should be protected by the same rights that govern already born humans.

This is the topic sentence of Paragraph 4. Without reading the rest of the paragraph, guess what it will be about.

This is a supporting detail. It helps prove the paragraph's topic sentence true.

"On the other hand" is a transitional phrase that keeps the ideas in the essay moving.

Paragraph 5

Is an embryo a full-fledged human person waiting to happen? Or is it, like an acorn and an oak tree, intricately related, yet fundamentally different? The question is highly personal, infinitely complicated, and has no correct answer. Americans will continue to explore what embryos mean to them and form opinions on stem cell research accordingly.

Note how the conclusion returns to the point made in the introduction without repeating material that came earlier.

Works Cited

Committee on Pro-Life Activities of the United States Conference of Catholic Bishops (USCCB). *On Embryonic Stem Cell Research*. Washington, DC: USCCB, June 2008.

Sandel, Michael J. "Examining the Ethics of Embryonic Stem Cell Research: A Conversation with HSCI's Michael J. Sandel." Harvard Stem Cell Institute. *Stem Cell Lines* Spring/Summer 2007.

Exercise 1A: Create an Outline from an Existing Essay

It often helps to create an outline of the five-paragraph essay before you write it. The outline can help you organize the information, arguments, and evidence you have gathered during your research.

For this exercise, create an outline that could have been used to write *Defining Embryos, Defining Values*. This "reverse engineering" exercise is meant to help familiarize you with how outlines can help classify and arrange information.

To do this you will need to
1. articulate the essay's thesis,
2. pinpoint important pieces of evidence,
3. flag quotes that supported the essay's ideas, and
4. identify key points that supported the argument.

Part of the outline has already been started to give you an idea of the assignment.

Outline
I. Paragraph 1
Write the essay's thesis:

II. Paragraph 2
Topic: People who oppose embryonic stem cell research define embryos as persons in a pre-infant state.

Supporting Detail i.

Supporting Detail ii. Quote by the United States Conference of Catholic Bishops arguing that embryos are people too.

III. Paragraph 3
Topic:

Supporting Detail i. The point that an embryo does not have a body or any body parts, cannot live on its own, and does not have the ability to hear, think, feel, or see.

Supporting Detail ii.

IV. **Paragraph 4**
Topic:

Supporting Detail i. Statistic from the Pew Research Center showing that the majority of Americans—56 percent—think it is more important to conduct stem cell research than to avoid destroying embryos used in the research.

Supporting Detail ii.

V. **Paragraph 5**
Write the essay's conclusion:

Support Ethical Stem Cell Research That Already Works

Editor's Notes One way of writing an expository essay is to use the problem/solution method. Problem/Solution refers to when the author raises a problem or a question, then uses the rest of the paragraph or essay to answer the question or provide possible resolutions to the problem. The following sample essay uses problem/solution to show how research on adult stem (AS) cells and induced pluripotent stem (iPS) cells can cure disease. The author describes the problem of disease, which plagues millions of American families each year. The author then uses the essay's supporting paragraphs to describe each of the ways in which AS and iPS cell research offers solutions to the problem posed.

Unlike the first model essay, this expository essay is also persuasive, meaning that the author wants to persuade you to agree with her point of view. As you read, keep track of the notes in the margins. They will help you analyze how the essay is organized and how it is written.

■ Refers to thesis and topic sentences

■ Refers to supporting details

Paragraph 1

Americans are increasingly living with disease: An estimated 80 million Americans have heart disease, and 910,000 die from it every year, making it the nation's number 1 killer. Sixty-six thousand Americans are believed to be living with multiple myeloma, and 20,000 will be diagnosed with this deadly bone cancer this year. An additional 250,000 suffer from spinal cord injuries. But what if there were a cure for these terrible diseases? What if there were a treatment to make their lives easier and less painful? The search for such

What problem is established in the introductory paragraph?

What is the essay's the- sis statement? How did you recognize it?

cures has led scientists to study stem cells extracted from human embryos. But two other kinds of stem cell research—research using adult stem cells (AS) and induced pluripotent stem cells (iPS), made from repro- grammed adult cells that act like embryonic cells—have already cured disease, and without the ethical compli- cations inherent in embryonic stem (ES) cell research. Because of this, Americans should put their money, time, and faith in AS and iPS research and abandon research involving ES cells.

Paragraph 2

This is the topic sen- tence of Paragraph 2. It is a subset of the essay's thesis.

Adult stem cell research should be supported primarily because it has already been proven to work. In fact, AS cells have been used to successfully treat more than eleven thousand Americans who suffer from dozens of illnesses, including cancer, spinal cord injuries, auto- immune diseases, cardiovascular disease, immunodefi- ciency disorders, sickle-cell anemia and other blood dis- orders, and neural degenerative disease. Furthermore,

This is a supporting detail. It helps prove the topic sentence true.

treatments involving adult stem cells have undergone more than two thousand clinical trials, tests that deter- mine a technology or treatment's safety and efficacy. ES cells, on the other hand, have not yet undergone any clinical trials, nor have they actually been used to suc- cessfully cure a single disease or disorder. "Researchers in embryonic stem cell research will tell you there is great promise and potential in their work," says col- umnist Bob Kemp. But "embryonic stem cell treatments have rendered no success stories at all; not even one. Patients treated with embryonic stem cells have their hopes crushed after having them built up so greatly by those they are led to put their trust in. Often times the patients will develop cancers or tumors as a direct result of embryonic stem cell treatments" (Kemp).

Paragraph 3

Another benefit of AS cells is that they are ready to use now; ES cells, however, still have yet to prove they are the miracle cure that everyone has hyped. In fact, not only have ES cells delivered no cures or treatments, experts believe it may be years before they do. Stem cell research experts such as James Thomson and Robert Winston have admitted that breakthroughs involving ES cells are decades, perhaps even centuries, away. Said Winston, "I am not entirely convinced that embryonic stem cells will, in my lifetime, and possibly anybody's lifetime for that matter, be holding quite the promise that we desperately hope they will" (Winston).

What point does this quote directly support?

Paragraph 4

Perhaps the best part about AS and iPS cell research is that neither raise the ethical complications that make ES cell research so controversial. In both AS and iPS cell research, there is no embryo. Cells are taken directly from patients who can give their consent, rather than their lives. Neither technology requires the destruction of human embryos, nor do they rely upon egg donations. Instead, adult stem cells are harvested from patients themselves, or from the cord blood of already born infants. This fact absolves them of any ethical complications, and for this reason alone their use should be encouraged over ES cells. Mike Pence, a Republican congressman from Indiana, agrees, saying, "Scientific breakthroughs [using adult stem cells] have rendered embryonic stem-cell research obsolete, effectively removing any perceived need to destroy human embryos in the name of science" (Pence).

This is the topic sentence of Paragraph 4. Without reading ahead, take a guess at what the rest of the paragraph will discuss.

Why do you think the author has included this information about Mike Pence?

Paragraph 5

Everyone wants to cure disease, but there is a right and a wrong way to go about doing so. We already have stem cell technology that offers cures to disease and upholds respect for human life. Why are we continuing to look for solutions in research that is significantly less ethical and holds significantly less promise?

This sentence is part of the author's attempt to persuade you to agree with her. What other persuasive sentences or phrases are found in the essay?

Works Cited

Kemp, Bob. "Embryonic Stem Cell Research: Bad Science Funded by the White House." Renew America.com 30 July 2009 < http://www.renewamerica.com/columns/kemp/090730 > .

Pence, Mike. "The Empty Promise of Embryonic Stem Cell Research." *Christianity Today* 23 Mar. 2009 < http://www.christianitytoday.com/ct/2009/marchweb-only/112-11.0.html?start = 1 > .

Winston, Robert. "Should We Trust the Scientists?" Lecture at Gresham College 20 June 2005 < http://www.gresham.ac.uk/printtranscript.asp?EventId = 347 > .

Exercise 2A: Create an Outline from an Existing Essay

As you did for the first model essay in this section, create an outline that could have been used to write "Support Ethical Stem Cell Research That Already Works." Be sure to identify the essay's thesis statement, its supporting ideas, its descriptive passages, and key pieces of evidence that were used.

Exercise 2B: Create an Outline for Your Own Essay

The second model essay expresses a particular point of view about stem cell research. For this exercise, your assignment is to find supporting ideas, choose specific and concrete details, create an outline, and ultimately write a five-paragraph essay making a different, or even opposing, point about stem cell research. Your goal is to use expository and persuasive techniques to convince your reader.

Part l: Write a thesis statement.

The following thesis statement would be appropriate for an opposing essay on why neither AS nor iPS cell research holds as much promise as ES cell research:

> *Once researchers discover how to unlock their power, embryonic stem cells promise to cure more diseases more effectively than AS and iPS cell research.*

Or see the sample paper topics suggested in Appendix D for more ideas.

Part II: Brainstorm pieces of supporting evidence.

Using information from some of the viewpoints in the previous section and from the information found in Section Three of this book, write down three arguments or pieces of evidence that support the thesis statement you selected. Then, for each of these three arguments, write down facts, examples, and details that support it. These could be:

- statistical and factual information;
- personal memories and anecdotes;
- quotes from experts, peers, or family members;
- observations of people's actions and behaviors;
- specific and concrete details.

Supporting pieces of evidence for the above sample thesis statement are found in this book and include:

- Points made in Viewpoint Four by the Coalition for the Advancement of Medical Research about how ES research led to the discovery of AS research, and that AS research has had very narrow success.
- Quote from Viewpoint Four about how iPS cell lines are less stable and safe than ES lines: "iPS cells are much further from the clinic than are ES cells. At present, they are made with genes and viruses that can cause cancer."
- Poll data that accompanies Viewpoint Four that show the majority of Americans—52 percent—support pursuing embryonic stem cell research without strict federal restrictions.

Part III: Place the information from Part II in outline form.

Part IV: Write the arguments or supporting statements in paragraph form.

By now you have three arguments that support the paragraph's thesis statement, as well as supporting material. Use the outline to write out your three supporting arguments in paragraph form. Make sure each paragraph has a topic sentence that states the paragraph's thesis clearly and broadly. Then, add supporting sentences that express the facts, quotes, details, and examples that support the paragraph's argument. The paragraph may also have a concluding or summary sentence.

A Use for Leftover Embryos

Essay
Three

Editor's Notes Yet another way of writing an expository essay is to use the process method. A process expository essay generally looks at how something is done. The writer presents events or steps in a chronological or other ordered sequence of steps. Process writing can either inform the reader of a past event or process by which something was made or accomplished, or instruct the reader on how to do something.

The following essay uses process to show how embryos created by in vitro fertilization end up being used for stem cell research. The author explains step-by-step how in vitro fertilization works, why and how some embryos go unused, how these are released to scientists for research, and what scientists hope to accomplish with them.

This essay differs from the previous model essays in that it is longer than five paragraphs. Sometimes five paragraphs are simply not enough to adequately develop an idea. Extending the length of an essay can allow the reader to explore a topic in more depth or present multiple pieces of evidence that together provide a complete picture of a topic. Longer essays can also help readers discover the complexity of a subject by examining a topic beyond its superficial exterior. Moreover, the ability to write a sustained research or position paper is a valuable skill you will need as you advance academically.

As you read, consider the questions posed in the margins. Continue to identify thesis statements, supporting details, transitions, and quotations. Examine the introductory and concluding paragraphs to understand how they give shape to the essay. Finally, evaluate the essay's general structure and assess its overall effectiveness.

Refers to thesis and topic sentences

Refers to supporting details

Paragraph 1

When a child-seeking couple cannot get pregnant naturally, they may seek out in vitro fertilization treatment (IVF), which allows egg fertilization and early embryo development to occur outside the body in a laboratory petri dish. IVF treatments sometimes produce miracle children born to grateful parents. More commonly they result in embryos that will not become children but can be donated to science. This essay will explore how in vitro fertilization works, why and how some embryos go unused, how these are released to scientists for research, and what scientists hope to accomplish with them.

Paragraph 2

First, women undergoing IVF are given medication—usually a type of hormone—that encourages their ovaries to develop and release viable, mature eggs. One of the reasons these women cannot get pregnant naturally is because their bodies have trouble doing this on their own. About thirty-six hours after the medication is given, the eggs are harvested from the woman. This is a delicate and tricky process that involves aspirating the eggs with a giant needle. The procedure is guided by ultrasound, which enables the physician to see where the needle is in the patient's body. As many as twenty-four eggs are harvested during this process.

What words and phrases let you know that this is a process essay?

Paragraph 3

Once extracted, the eggs are separated from other biological matter and examined to make sure they are healthy. Next they are put in a petri dish along with sperm. Fertilization then takes place in this dish, outside the parents. (Sometimes sperm are injected directly into an egg if the reason the couple cannot conceive is due to low sperm count or poor sperm motility, or movement.) If everything goes well, the eggs are fertilized within eighteen hours. Within twenty-four to seventy-two hours, the fertilized eggs have begun rapidly dividing and are now called embryos. These embryos are placed in a growth serum and incubator that keeps them alive while they continue to develop.

Paragraph 4

After about five days, the embryos have divided to the point where they are now referred to as blastocysts. These are highly divided groups of one hundred to two hundred cells that are ready for implantation in the uterine wall. They are only about the size of the period at the end of this sentence, but blastocysts contain the highly valuable undifferentiated, or pluripotent, stem cells that have the potential to turn into any organ cell in the body. Once the embryos have reached the blastocyst stage of development, they are prepared for transfer into the woman, where it is hoped they will attach to her uterus and start a pregnancy.

> What facts and statistics are used in the essay? Make a list of all facts and statistics and what points they are used in support of.

Paragraph 5

Before implantation, each embryo is examined to see if it is viable. Sometimes embryos are not selected for implantation because they have not developed normally or appear to carry genetic defects. Still other embryos are viable and healthy but are not implanted to avoid impregnating the woman with triplets, quadruplets, or quintuplets. Of all the embryos, the doctor will select just a couple of the best ones for implantation and set the rest aside.

Paragraph 6

The couple seeking IVF has now hopefully become pregnant, and the remaining embryos that have been set aside have three fates. They are either discarded, stored for potential future use, or donated to research. The process of discarding the embryos is straightforward and simple. Some are flushed down a sink or incinerated along with other medical waste. Some are allowed to die by leaving them exposed to the air, a process that takes about four days. Although these methods may sound cruel, the embryos feel no pain because they are, at this stage of development, simply a cluster of cells. They do not yet have a nervous system, limbs, a brain, eyes, consciousness, or any other features that would allow them to be aware of what is happening or experience any discomfort.

If embryos are not discarded, they are stored for potential future use by the couple who created them or, if the couple wishes, by another couple seeking to conceive. The embryos slated for future use are deep-frozen in liquid nitrogen in a process called "cryopreservation." According to a comprehensive survey undertaken by the Rand Corporation, more than four hundred thousand embryos are frozen in clinics around the United States. Some have been there since the late 1970s. Even if people never use their frozen embryos, they often feel great attachment to them. For example, Kim and Walt Best, of Tennessee, pay about two hundred dollars a year to keep nine embryos frozen at a fertility clinic at Duke University. The embryos were created when the Bests used IVF treatment to conceive twin girls. The remaining embryos were stored in case the original treatment did not work, and Kim Best thinks of them as her potential children, too. "I can't look at my twins and not wonder sometimes what the other nine would be like," she says (qtd. in Grady).

How does the quote from Kim Best help underscore the point being made in this paragraph? What is compelling about the quote?

But others who have leftover embryos choose to donate them to science—specifically, to stem cell research. Not all fertility clinics offer this option, but many couples who have recently undergone IVF treatment would choose it if they could, according to a 2008 study published by Duke University researchers in the journal *Fertility and Sterility*. The study found that 66 percent of patients who had finished fertility treatment said they would be somewhat likely or very likely to consider donating their embryos to stem cell research, if only their fertility clinic offered that option (just four of the nine clinics in the survey did). Only 12 percent of people who had recently undergone fertility treatments said they preferred to discard the embryos rather than donate them to science or to another couple trying to conceive. Study participant Jacqueline Betancourt explained that donating her embryos to sci-

What transitional words and phrases does the author use to keep the ideas in the essay smoothly flowing?

ence seemed like the best way to avoid wasting them. "The thought of throwing an embryo away just isn't a pleasant thought," Betancourt said. "Given all the developments you hear about with stem cell research, it felt like that truly was a potential good for society" (qtd. in Collins).

Paragraph 9

Couples like the Betancourts who choose to donate their leftover embryos are protected from being taken advantage of in several ways. For example, in order to donate leftover embryos, a couple must sign a consent form that turns the embryos over to the research laboratory. Such facilities are not allowed to offer financial incentives or other rewards to entice people to donate embryos, nor are they allowed to give preferential care or treatment to donating couples. In addition, to avoid a conflict of interest, the doctor who heads the in vitro fertilization treatments is not allowed to be the same person who would conduct research on any donated embryos. Finally, the couple is required to sign forms that state their donation is voluntary, that they understand the resulting research may or may not result in any medical breakthroughs, that they are aware that the stem cell lines created from their cells will exist for many years, and that the research and benefits derived from them may possibly be sold or otherwise commercialized.

Paragraph 10

Once it is donated, researchers take the embryo and try to harvest from it the valuable stem cells. This process kills the embryo but has the potential to create a long-lasting line of stem cells that can be used to understand how the body takes these undifferentiated cells and creates from them kidneys, skin, eyes, and every other body part. A 2008 study by Harvard researchers found that success in creating stem cell lines from donated embryos depends in large part on how old the embryos are. The younger an embryo, the fewer ethical issues result from its use; but

> Why do you think the author decided to include this quote in the essay? What point does it support? Who is the speaker, and how is that person relevant to the essay?

> What is the topic sentence of Paragraph 9? How did you recognize it?

> What is the topic sentence of Paragraph 10? How does it relate to the rest of the essay?

the older the embryo, the more likely it is that scientists can create a viable stem cell line. The Harvard researchers found it possible to create stem cell lines from three-day-old embryos, but only at a success rate of 0.6 percent. Five-day-old embryos, however, gave rise to stem cell lines at a rate of 4.1 percent, while those that had already developed into blastocysts yielded an 8.5 percent success rate. From these lines it is hoped that cures for a myriad of diseases and disorders will be found, including Parkinson's, Alzheimer's, and diabetes.

Paragraph 11

Performing research on leftover embryos from in vitro fertilization treatments—in fact, the very process of creating them at all—is frowned upon by some Americans but enthusiastically supported by others. As federal restrictions on stem cell research ease, it is likely that more clinics will offer the option of donating leftover embryos to science. Whether scientists will be able to discover the cures they hope to, however, remains to be seen.

Works Cited

Collins, Kristin. "Couples in US Prefer to Donate Embryos for Research, Study Finds." *McClatchy Newspapers* 4 Dec. 2008 < http://www.geneticsandsociety.org/article.php ?id = 4410 >.

Grady, Denise. "Parents Torn over Fate of Frozen Embryos." *New York Times* 4 Dec. 2008 < http://www.ny times.com/2008/12/04/us/04embryo.html?page wanted = 1 >.

Exercise 3A: Examining Introductions and Conclusions

Every essay features introductory and concluding paragraphs that are used to frame the main ideas being presented. Along with presenting the essay's thesis statement, well-written introductions should grab the attention of the reader and make clear why the topic being explored is important. The conclusion reiterates the essay's thesis and is also the last chance for the writer to make an impression on the reader. Strong introductions and conclusions can greatly enhance an essay's effect on an audience.

The Introduction

There are several techniques that can be used to craft an introductory paragraph. An essay can start with

- an anecdote: a brief story that illustrates a point relevant to the topic;
- startling information: facts or statistics that elucidate the point of the essay;
- setting up and knocking down a position: a position or claim believed by proponents of one side of a controversy, followed by statements that challenge that claim;
- historical perspective: an example of the way things used to be that leads into a discussion of how or why things work differently now;
- summary information: general introductory information about the topic that feeds into the essay's thesis statement.

1. Reread the introductory paragraphs of the model essays and of the viewpoints in Section One. Identify which of the techniques described above are used in the example essays. How do they grab the attention of the reader? Are their thesis statements clearly presented?
2. Write an introduction for the essay you have outlined and partially written in Exercise 2B using one of the techniques described above.

The Conclusion

The conclusion brings the essay to a close by summarizing or returning to its main ideas. Good conclusions, however, go beyond simply repeating these ideas. Strong conclusions explore a topic's broader implications and reiterate why it is important to consider. They may frame the essay by returning to an anecdote featured in the opening paragraph. Or, they may close with a quotation or refer back to an event in the essay. In opinionated essays, the conclusion can reiterate which side the essay is taking or ask the reader to reconsider a previously held position on the subject.

3. Reread the concluding paragraphs of the model essays and of the viewpoints in Section One. Which were most effective in driving their arguments home to the reader? What sorts of techniques did they use to do this? Did they appeal emotionally to the reader, or bookend an idea or event referenced elsewhere in the essay?

4. Write a conclusion for the essay you have outlined and partially written in Exercise 2B using one of the techniques described above.

Exercise 3B: Using Quotations to Enliven Your Essay

No essay is complete without quotations. Get in the habit of using quotes to support at least some of the ideas in your essays. Quotes do not need to appear in every paragraph, but often enough so that the essay contains voices aside from your own. When you write, use quotations to accomplish the following:

- Provide expert advice that you are not necessarily in the position to know about.
- Cite lively or passionate passages.
- Include a particularly well-written point that gets to the heart of the matter.

- Supply statistics or facts that have been derived from someone's research.
- Deliver anecdotes that illustrate the point you are trying to make.
- Express first-person testimony.

Problem One:
Reread the essays presented in all sections of this book and find at least one example of each of the above quotation types.

There are a couple of important things to remember when using quotations:

- Note your sources' qualifications and biases. This way your reader can identify the person you have quoted and can put their words in a context.
- Put any quoted material within proper quotation marks. Failing to attribute quotes to their authors constitutes plagiarism, which is when an author takes someone else's words or ideas and presents them as their own. Plagiarism is a very serious infraction and must be avoided at all costs.

Using the information from this book, write your own five-paragraph expository essay that deals with stem cell research. You can use the resources in this book for information about issues relating to this topic and how to structure this type of essay.

The following steps are suggestions on how to get started.

Step One: Choose your topic.

The first step is to decide what topic to write your expository essay on. Is there any subject that particularly fascinates you about stem cell research? Is there an aspect of the topic you strongly support, or feel strongly against? Is there an issue you feel personally connected to or one that you would like to learn more about? Ask yourself such questions before selecting your essay topic. Refer to Appendix D: Sample Essay Topics if you need help selecting a topic.

Step Two: Write down questions and answers about the topic.

Before you begin writing, you will need to think carefully about what ideas your essay will contain. This is a process known as *brainstorming*. Brainstorming involves asking yourself questions and coming up with ideas to discuss in your essay. Possible questions that will help you with the brainstorming process include:

- Why is this topic important?
- Why should people be interested in this topic?
- How can I make this essay interesting to the reader?
- What question am I going to address in this paragraph or essay?
- What facts, ideas, or quotes can I use to support the answer to my question?

Questions especially for persuasive essays include:

- Do I want to write an informative essay or an opinionated essay?

- Will I need to explain a process or course of action?
- Will my essay contain many definitions or explanations?
- Is there a particular problem that needs to be solved?

Step Three: Gather facts, ideas, and anecdotes related to your topic.

This book contains several places to find information about many issues relating to stem cell research, including the viewpoints and the appendices. In addition, you may want to research the books, articles, and Web sites listed in Section Three, or do additional research in your local library. You can also conduct interviews if you know someone who has a compelling story that would fit well in your essay.

Step Four: Develop a workable, thesis statement.

Use what you have written down in steps two and three to help you articulate the main point or argument you want to make in your essay. It should be expressed in a clear sentence and make an arguable or supportable point.

Example:

Embryos are humans, too, and it is wrong to sacrifice their lives in the pursuit of the health of others. This could be the thesis statement of an expository essay that illustrates all the reasons why the author thinks embryonic stem cell research is immoral.

Step Five: Write an outline or diagram.
1. Write the thesis statement at the top of the outline.
2. Write roman numerals I, II, and III on the left side of the page with A, B, and C under each numeral.
3. Next to each roman numeral, write down the best ideas you came up with in step three. These should all directly relate to and support the thesis statement.
4. Next to each letter write down information that supports that particular idea.

Step Six: Write the three supporting paragraphs.
Use your outline to write the three supporting paragraphs. Write down the main idea of each paragraph in sentence form. Do the same thing for the supporting points of information. Each sentence should support the paragraph of the topic. Be sure you have relevant and interesting details, facts, and quotes. Use transitions when you move from idea to idea to keep the text fluid and smooth. Sometimes, although not always, paragraphs can include a concluding or summary sentence that restates the paragraph's argument.

Step Seven: Write the introduction and conclusion.
See Exercise 3A for information on writing introductions and conclusions.

Step Eight: Read and rewrite.
As you read, check your essay for the following:

- ✔ Does the essay maintain a consistent tone?
- ✔ Do all paragraphs reinforce your general thesis?
- ✔ Do all paragraphs flow from one to the other? Do you need to add transition words or phrases?
- ✔ Have you quoted from reliable, authoritative, and interesting sources?
- ✔ Is there a sense of progression throughout the essay?
- ✔ Does the essay get bogged down in too much detail or irrelevant material?
- ✔ Does your introduction grab the reader's attention?
- ✔ Does your conclusion reflect back on any previously discussed material, or give the essay a sense of closure?
- ✔ Are there any spelling or grammatical errors?

Section Three: Supporting Research Material

Facts About Stem Cell Research

Editor's Note: These facts can be used in reports to reinforce or add credibility when making important points or claims.

Important Dates in Stem Cell Research

1963
Self-renewing cells are discovered in the bone marrow of mice.

1968
Bone marrow transplant between two siblings successfully treats severe combined immunodeficiency (SCID).

1978
Hematopoietic stem cells (which are responsible for creating all components of blood cells) are discovered in human cord blood.

July 1978
The first test-tube baby is born. Louise Brown becomes the first baby in the world to be conceived by in vitro fertilization (IVF).

1981
Embryonic stem cells are culled from the inner cell mass of mice. The term "embryonic stem cell" is coined by scientist Gail Martin.

March 1984
Australian Zoe Leyland is the first baby born from a frozen IVF embryo.

1992
Neural stem cells are cultured in vitro.

1997
Leukemia is found to originate in hematopoietic stem cells—the first direct evidence of cancerous stem cells.

November 1998
The first human embryonic stem cell line is derived at the University of Wisconsin–Madison by James Thomson and colleagues.

2001
The first early (four- to six-cell stage) human embryos are cloned at Advanced Cell Technology for the purpose of generating embryonic stem cells.

August 2001
President George W. Bush limits federal funding of embryonic stem cell research to lines that were derived prior to the signing of his executive order.

March 2004
Korean researcher Hwang Woo Suk claims to have created an embryonic stem cell line through cloning, without the use of an embryo. The research is later revealed to be fabricated.

November 2004
Frustrated with the Bush Administration limits on stem cell research funding, Californians vote to allocate $3 billion over ten years to stem cell research.

2005
Researchers at Kingston University in England discover cord blood–derived embryonic-like stem cells (CBEs), found in umbilical cord blood. These cells are able to differentiate into more types of tissue than adult stem cells.

July 2006
President George W. Bush vetoes a bill that would allow federal funding for stem cell research on embryos discarded by IVF patients.

August 2006
Kazutoshi Takahashi and Shinya Yamanaka discover pluripotent stem cells can be induced in rats.

October 2006
Scientists in England create the first ever artificial liver cells using umbilical cord blood stem cells.

June 2007
Normal skin cells are found to be capable of being reprogrammed to an embryonic state in mice.

October 2007
Mario Capecchi, Martin Evans, and Oliver Smithies win the 2007 Nobel Prize for Physiology or Medicine for their work on mouse embryonic stem cells.

November 2007
Human induced pluripotent stem (iPS) cells are created, making it possible to produce a stem cell from almost any other human cell instead of relying on embryos.

January 2009
Biotech company Geron announces that it has received Food and Drug Administration clearance to launch the world's first human embryonic-stem-cell clinical trial.

March 2009
President Barack Obama signs an executive order lifting the Bush Administration's limitations on embryonic stem cell research. The National Institutes of Health (NIH) crafts new draft guidelines for scientists.

December 2009
The NIH approves forty embryonic stem cell lines available for federally funded research.

Facts About Different Kinds of Stem Cells
Embryonic stem cells are extracted from a blastocyst, a cluster of 180–200 cells approximately one-tenth the size of the head of a pin.

An embryo does not have a body or any body parts, and it does not have the ability to see, hear, feel, or think.

According to the Right to Life Organization, no human has ever successfully been treated with embryonic stem cells.

According to the National Institutes of Health, adult stem cells found in bone marrow have been used to treat leukemia, lymphoma, and several inherited blood disorders for over forty years.

According to the International Cord Blood Society over seventy diseases can be treated with stem cells derived from umbilical cord blood.

According to the New York Stem Cell Foundation, reprogrammed adult stem cells (iPS cells) are created with genes and retroviruses that can cause cancer in humans.

American Opinions on Stem Cell Research
An annual poll taken by Gallup organization reveals the following about American opinions about the morality of embryonic stem cell research:

- In 2009, 57 percent of Americans thought it was morally acceptable to conduct medical research on stem cells obtained from human embryos; 36 percent did not.

- In 2008, 62 percent thought it was morally acceptable; 30 percent did not; the rest were unsure.
- In 2007, 64 percent thought it was morally acceptable; 30 percent did not; the rest were unsure.
- In 2006, 61 percent thought it was morally acceptable; 30 percent did not; the rest were unsure.
- In 2003, 54 percent thought it was morally acceptable; 38 percent did not; the rest were unsure.

A 2008 poll by *Time* found that:

- 73 percent of Americans favor using embryos discarded from in vitro fertilization in stem cell research;
- 19 percent oppose it;
- 8 percent are unsure.

A 2009 Gallup poll found that:

- 14 percent of Americans favor having no restrictions on government funding of stem cell research;
- 38 percent favor easing restrictions;
- 22 percent favor imposing some restrictions;
- 19 percent oppose all federal funding of stem cell research;
- 7 percent are unsure.

A 2007 poll by the Pew Research Center asked Americans which was more important to them: conducting stem cell research that might result in new medical cures, or preserving the potential life of human embryos involved in the research? The poll revealed:

- 51 percent of Americans thought it was more important to conduct stem cell research;
- 35 percent thought it was more important to not destroy potential life;
- 14 percent were unsure.

Finding and Using Sources of Information

No matter what type of essay you are writing, it is necessary to find information to support your point of view. You can use sources such as books, magazine articles, newspaper articles, and online articles.

Using Books and Articles

You can find books and articles in a library by using the library's computer or cataloging system. If you are not sure how to use these resources, ask a librarian to help you. You can also use a computer to find many magazine articles and other articles written specifically for the Internet.

You are likely to find a lot more information than you can possibly use in your essay, so your first task is to narrow it down to what is likely to be most usable. Look at book and article titles. Look at book chapter titles, and examine the book's index to see if it contains information on the specific topic you want to write about. (For example, if you want to write about the effect of social media on Americans' lives and you find a book about the Internet in general, check the chapter titles and index to be sure it contains information relevant to your topic before you bother to check out the book.)

For a five-paragraph essay, you do not need a great deal of supporting information, so quickly try to narrow down your materials to a few good books and magazine or Internet articles. You do not need dozens. You might even find that one or two good books or articles contain all the information you need.

You probably do not have time to read an entire book, so find the chapters or sections that relate to your topic, and skim these. When you find useful information, copy it onto a note card or notebook. You should look for supporting facts, statistics, quotations, and examples.

Using the Internet

When you select your supporting information, it is important that you evaluate its source. This is especially important with information you find on the Internet. Because nearly anyone can put information on the Internet, there is as much bad information as good information. Before using Internet information—or any information—try to determine whether the source seems to be reliable. Is the author or Internet site sponsored by a legitimate organization? Is it from a government source? Does the author have any special knowledge or training relating to the topic you are looking up? Does the article give any indication of where its information comes from?

Using Your Supporting Information

When you use supporting information from a book, article, interview or other source, there are three important things to remember:

1. *Make it clear whether you are using a direct quotation or a paraphrase.* If you copy information directly from your source, you are quoting it. You must put quotation marks around the information, and tell where the information comes from. If you put the information in your own words, you are paraphrasing it.

Here is an example of a using a quotation:

> Because it relies on the destruction of human embryos, stem cell research is a morally questionable practice. Writer and lawyer Wesley J. Smith put it best when he described embryonic stem cell research as "a launching pad to an ever-deepening erosion of the unique moral status of human life."

Here is an example of a brief paraphrase of the same passage:

> Because it relies on the destruction of human embryos, stem cell research is a morally questionable practice. It is a starting point for accepting deeper and deeper assaults on the sanctity of human life. After all, once we embrace the destruction of embryos for the sake of science, what is to stop us from destroying fetuses, and then even infants, in the same pursuit?

2. *Use the information fairly*. Be careful to use supporting information in the way the author intended it. Avoid taking information out of context or using evidence unfairly.

3. *Give credit where credit is due*. Giving credit is known as citing. You must use citations when you use someone else's information, but not every piece of supporting information needs a citation.
   - If the supporting information is general knowledge—that is, it can be found in many sources—you do not have to cite your source.
   - If you directly quote a source, you must cite it.
   - If you paraphrase information from a specific source, you must cite it.

If you do not use citations where you should, you are *plagiarizing*—or stealing—someone else's work.

Citing Your Sources

There are a number of ways to cite your sources. Your teacher will probably want you to do it in one of three ways:

- Informal: As in the example in number 1 above, tell where you got the information as you present it in the text of your essay.
- Informal list: At the end of your essay, place an unnumbered list of all the sources you used. This

tells the reader where, in general, your information came from.

- Formal: Use numbered footnotes or endnotes. Footnotes or endnotes are generally placed at the end of an article or essay, although they may be placed elsewhere depending on your teacher's requirements.

Works Cited

Smith, Wesley J. "Stem Cell Debate Is Over Ethics, Not Science." *Orthodoxy Today* 23 Mar. 2009 < http://www .orthodoxytoday.org/articles-2009/Smith-Stem-Cell-Debate-Is-Over-Ethics-Not-Science.php > .

Using MLA Style to Create a Works Cited List

You will probably need to create a list of works cited for your paper. These include materials that you quoted from, relied heavily on, or consulted to write your paper. There are several different ways to structure these references. The following examples are based on Modern Language Association (MLA) style, one of the major citation styles used by writers.

Book Entries

For most book entries you will need the author's name, the book's title, where it was published, what company published it, and the year it was published. This information is usually found on the inside of the book. Variations on book entries include the following:

A book by a single author:
> Axworthy, Michael. *A History of Iran: Empire of the Mind.* New York: Basic Books, 2008.

Two or more books by the same author:
> Pollan, Michael. *In Defense of Food: An Eater's Manifesto.* New York: Penguin, 2009.
> ———. *The Omnivore's Dilemma.* New York: Penguin, 2006.

A book by two or more authors:
> Ronald, Pamela C., and R.W. Adamchak. *Tomorrow's Table: Organic Farming, Genetics, and the Future of Food.* New York: Oxford University Press, 2008.

A book with an editor:
> Friedman, Lauri S., ed. *Introducing Issues with Opposing Viewpoints: War.* Detroit: Greenhaven, 2009.

Periodical and Newspaper Entries

Entries for sources found in periodicals and newspapers are cited a bit differently than books. For one, these sources usually have a title and a publication name. They also may have specific dates and page numbers. Unlike book entries, you do not need to list where newspapers or periodicals are published or what company publishes them.

An article from a periodical:
> Hannum, William H., Gerald E. Marsh, and George S. Stanford. "Smarter Use of Nuclear Waste," *Scientific American* Dec. 2005: 84–91.

An unsigned article from a periodical:
> Chinese Disease? The Rapid Spread of Syphilis in China." *Global Agenda* 14 Jan. 2007.

An article from a newspaper:
> Weiss, Rick. "Can Food from Cloned Animals Be Called Organic?" *Washington Post* 29 Jan. 2008: A06.

Internet Sources

To document a source you found online, try to provide as much information on it as possible, including the author's name, the title of the document, date of publication or of last revision, the URL, and your date of access.

A Web source:
> De Seno, Tommy. *"Roe vs. Wade* and the Rights of the Father." Fox Forum.com 22 Jan. 2009 < http://fox forum.blogs.foxnews.com/2009/01/22/deseno_ roe_wade > .

Your teacher will tell you exactly how information should be cited in your essay. Generally, the very least information needed is the original author's name and the name of the article or other publication.

Be sure you know exactly what information your teacher requires before you start looking for your supporting information so that you know what information to include with your notes.

Appendix D

Sample Essay Topics

The Definition of a Stem Cell

Explaining the Ins and Outs of Somatic Cell Nuclear Transfer (SCNT)

Types of Stem Cells

New Advances in Stem Cell Research

A History of Stem Cell Research

The Difference Between Reproductive Cloning and Therapeutic Cloning: Is There One?

What Kinds of Cells Might Replace the Need for Embryos in Research?

Embryonic Stem Cell Research Is Immoral

Embryonic Stem Cell Research Is Moral

Embryos Used in Stem Cell Research Are Human Beings

Embryos Used in Stem Cell Research Are Not Yet Human Beings

Embryonic Stem Cell Research Amounts to Murder

Embryonic Stem Cell Research Is Not Murder

Discarded IVF Embryos Should Be Donated to Stem Cell Researchers

Discarded IVF Embryos Should Not Be Donated to Stem Cell Researchers

Frozen IVF Embryos Should Be Donated to Couples Seeking Children

Embryonic Stem Cell Research Can Cure Many Diseases

The Curative Power of Embryonic Stem Cells Has Been Exaggerated

Alternatives to Embryonic Stem Cell Research Can Cure Disease

Alternatives to Embryonic Stem Cell Research Cannot Effectively Cure Disease

Embryonic Stem Cell Research Is Necessary to Find a Cure for Diabetes

A Cure for Diabetes Can Be Found Through Nonembryonic Stem Cell Research

Embryonic Stem Cell Research Can Someday Cure Alzheimer's Disease

Embryonic Stem Cell Research Is Unlikely to Ever Cure Alzheimer's Disease

Embryonic Stem Cell Research Can Someday Cure Parkinson's Disease

Embryonic Stem Cell Research Is Unlikely to Ever Cure Parkinson's Disease

Stem Cells Made from Skin Are Effective

Stem Cells Made from Skin Are Not Effective

Stem Cells Made from Adult Cells Are Effective

Stem Cells Made from Adult Cells Are Not Effective

The Government Should Fund Stem Cell Research

The Government Should Not Fund Stem Cell Research

State Governments Will Fund Stem Cell Research If the Federal Government Does Not

The Number of Federally Approved Stem Cell Lines Should Be Increased

The Number of Federally Approved Stem Cell Lines Should Not Be Increased

Americans Favor Government Support of Human Embryonic Stem Cell Research

Americans Do Not Favor Government Support of Human Embryonic Stem Cell Research

Stem Cell Research Policies Hurt the United States

Stem Cell Research Policies Do Not Hurt the United States

Stem Cell Research Will Lead to Human Cloning

Stem Cell Research Will Not Lead to Human Cloning

Glossary

adult stem cells: Also called somatic stem cells, these are nonembryonic stem cells that are not derived from gametes (egg or sperm cells). They are body cells that can give rise to the specialized cell types of the tissue from which they came. For example, a blood stem cell can give rise to all the cells that make up the blood but not the cells of other organs, such as the liver or skin.

blastocyst: A very early-developed ball-shaped embryo that consists of approximately one hundred to two hundred cells; what embryonic stem cells are harvested from.

cell line: Cells capable of reproducing themselves while maintained in culture.

differentiation: The process by which an embryonic cell acquires the features of a specialized cell such as those found in heart, liver, or muscle tissue.

Dolly the sheep: The first mammal to be cloned using nuclear transfer.

embryo: The earliest stages of a human being; the period of development between the fertilized egg and the fetal stage, from conception to about eight weeks gestation.

embryonic stem cell: Cells derived from a five-day-old embryo prior to implantation in the uterus. They have the potential to become a wide variety of specialized cell types. They are self-renewing (can replicate themselves) and are pluripotent (have the ability to form all cell types found in the body).

human embryonic stem cell research: Research on stem cells extracted from human embryos.

induced pluripotent stem cell: Specialized cells such as skin cells that have been engineered, or reprogrammed, to act like pluripotent embryonic stem cell.

in vitro fertilization: A technique that unites the egg and sperm in a laboratory instead of inside the female body.

pluripotent stem cells: Stem cells that have the ability to become any type of cell found in the body.

reproductive cloning: The creation of a baby through nuclear transfer. The cloned individual would be genetically identical to the donor of the nucleus.

somatic cell nuclear transfer (SCNT): The replacement of genetic material (nuclear DNA) in an unfertilized egg with genetic material from an adult somatic cell (such as a skin cell).

therapeutic cloning: The use of cloning technology to help in the search for possible cures and treatments for diseases and disabilities.

undifferentiated: A cell that has not yet generated structures or manufactured proteins characteristic of a specialized cell type; has the potential to turn into any kind of body cell.

Organizations to Contact

The editor has compiled the following list of organizations concerned with the issues debated in this book. The descriptions are derived from materials provided by the organizations. All have publications or information available for interested readers. The list was compiled on the date of publication of the present volume; the information provided here may change. Be aware that many organizations take several weeks or longer to respond to queries, so allow as much time as possible.

American Association for the Advancement of Science (AAAS)
1200 New York Ave. NW, Washington, DC 20005
(202) 326-6400 • e-mail: webmaster@aaas.org
Web site: www.aaas.org

This international nonprofit organization serves as an educator, leader, spokesperson, and professional association dedicated to advancing science around the world. It publishes the journal *Science* as well as many scientific newsletters, books, and reports. A search of "stem cell research" on its Web site yields numerous articles and publications.

American Life League (ALL)
PO Box 1350, Stafford, VA 22555 • (540) 659-4171
fax: (540) 659-2586 • e-mail: info@all.org
Web site: www.all.org

ALL is an educational pro-life organization that opposes abortion, artificial contraception, reproductive technologies, and fetal experimentation. It asserts that to perform experiments on living human embryos and fetuses is immoral, whether inside or outside of the mother's womb. Its publications include the brochures *Stem Cell Research: The Science of Human Sacrifice* and *Human Cloning: The Science of Deception*.

American Medical Association (AMA)
515 N. State St., Chicago, IL 60610 • (800) 621-8335
Web site: www.ama-assn.org

The AMA is the largest professional association for medical doctors. It helps set standards for medical education and practices, and it is a powerful lobby in Washington for physicians' interests. The association publishes an e-newsletter as well as journals for many medical fields, including the weekly *JAMA*. Searching for "stem cells" on its Web site retrieves numerous articles about stem cell research.

The Center for Bioethics & Human Dignity
2065 Half Day Rd., Deerfield, IL 60015 • (847) 317-8180
fax: (847) 317-8101 • e-mail: info@cbhd.org
Web site: www.cbhd.org

Formed in 1994 by Christian bioethicists, CBHD is a nonprofit international organization that strives to provide research, publications, and teaching to engage leaders in bioethics. The center has initiated a number of projects, including Do No Harm: The Coalition of Americans for Research Ethics, a partnership of researchers, bioethicists, academics, and others that serves as an information clearinghouse on the ethics and science of stem cell research. CBHD maintains the Do No Harm Web site, which advocates for adult stem cell research and other medical technologies that do not involve the destruction of human embryos.

Christian Coalition of America
PO Box 37030, Washington, DC 20013-7030
(202) 479-6900 • fax: (202) 479-4260
Web site: www.cc.org

The Christian Coalition of America is a conservative grass-roots political organization that offers Christians a vehicle to become actively involved in shaping their local and national governments. It represents a pro-family agenda and works to educate America about critical issues, including opposing the destruction of human embryos through stem cell research. The Web site provides action alerts, a weekly newsletter, commentary, and voter education information that encourages citizens to vote.

Coalition for the Advancement of Medical Research (CAMR)

2021 K St. NW, Suite 305, Washington, DC 20006
(202) 725-0339 • e-mail: camresearch@yahoo.com
Web site: www.camradvocacy.org

CAMR is a bipartisan coalition composed of more than one hundred nationally recognized patient organizations, universities, scientific societies, and foundations. CAMR focuses on developing better treatments and cures for individuals with life-threatening illnesses and disorders. It periodically performs polls to gauge American response to stem cell research, and its Web site provides links to the publications reporting on the most recent developments and events related to stem cell research.

Concerned Women for America (CWA)

1015 Fifteenth St. NW, Suite 1100, Washington, DC 20005
(202) 488-7000 • fax: (202) 488-0806
Web site: www.cwfa.org

The CWA is a women's public policy organization that aims to bring the principles of the bible into all levels of public policy and to restore the nation's moral values. CWA focuses on preserving traditional family values as well protecting the sanctity of human life. As a result, it opposes embryonic stem cell research. Its Web site has article links, press releases, and legislative alerts on this topic.

Council for Responsible Genetics (CRG)

5 Upland Rd., Suite 3, Cambridge, MA 02140
(617) 868-0870 • fax: (617) 491-5344
e-mail: crg@gene-watch.org
Web site: www.councilforresponsiblegenetics.org

CRG is a national nonprofit, nongovernmental organization of scientists, health professionals, trade unionists, women's health activists, and others who work to ensure that genetic technologies are developed safely and in the best interest of the public. The council publishes the bimonthly newsletter *GeneWatch* and has several programs that address specific genetics-related issues, including a program called Human Genetic Manipulation and Cloning.

Family Research Council

801 G St. NW, Washington, DC 20001 • (202) 393-2100
fax: (202) 393-2134 •Web site: www.frc.org

The Family Research Council is a Christian right nonprofit think tank and lobbying organization that promotes the traditional family unit based on Judeo-Christian values. It advocates for national policies that protect traditional notions of marriage and family and the sanctity of human life via books, pamphlets, public events, debates, and testimony. One of its central focuses is on human life and bioethics, and it opposes research that harms, manipulates, or destroys an embryonic human being and vigorously supports adult stem cell therapies that can treat patients.

Focus on the Family

8605 Explorer Dr., Colorado Springs, CO 80920
(800) 232-6459 • Web site: www.focusonthefamily.com

Focus on the Family promotes a socially conservative public policy. As such, it opposes any activity it deems a threat to the traditional idea of family, including embryonic stem cell research. The organization provides free family counseling, a variety of a publications it deems important to family values, and a radio broadcast that reaches 220 million listeners daily in 160 countries.

Genetics Policy Institute (GPI)

11924 Forest Hill Blvd., Suite 22, Wellington, FL 33414
(888) 238-1423 • fax: (561) 791-3889
Web site: www.genpol.org

The Genetics Policy Institute is the leading nonprofit organization dedicated to establishing a positive legal framework to advance stem cell research. GPI maintains science and legal advisory boards composed of leading stem cell researchers, disease experts, ethicists, and legal experts, and a dedicated full-time staff of policy experts that are available to educate the public and media on stem cell issues.

Harvard Stem Cell Institute (HSCI)

42 Church St., Cambridge, MA 02138 • (617) 496-4050
e-mail: hsci@harvard.edu
Web site: www.hsci.harvard.edu

The HSCI, composed of Harvard Medical School and eighteen hospitals and research institutions, hosts one of the largest concentrations of biomedical researchers in the world. Its newsletter *Stem Cell Lines* is published three times per year, its monthly newsletter publishes the scientific work of its faculty, and it offers scientific overviews that focus on the use of stem cells and potential therapeutic applications. Topics covered include stem cells and diseases, stem cells and neurodegenerative disease, and type 1 diabetes.

The Hastings Center

21 Malcolm Gordon Rd., Garrison, NY 10524-4125
(845) 424-4040 • fax: (845) 424-4545
e-mail: mail@thehastingscenter.org
Web site: www.thehastingscenter.org

The Hastings Center is an independent, nonpartisan, and nonprofit bioethics research institute. Since its founding in 1969, the center has played a central role in responding to advances in medicine, the biological sciences, and the social sciences by raising ethical questions related to such advances, including stem cell research. The center publishes books, papers, guidelines, and the bimonthly *Hastings Center Report*.

Institute for Stem Cell Research
School of Biological Sciences, The University of Edinburgh, The Roger Land Building, The King's Buildings
West Mains Rd., Edinburgh, Scotland EH9 3JQ
+44 (0)131 650 5828 • fax: +44 (0)131 650 7773
e-mail: p.hope@ed.ac.uk
Web site: www.iscr.ed.ac.uk

The Institute for Stem Cell Research is a global stem cell research and technology center devoted to developing stem cell therapies that can be used to treat human injury and disease. The center hosts state-of-the-art research and laboratory facilities to accommodate research in stem cell culture and experimental embryology. It also offers regular seminar series, and its Web site provides links to many institutes performing stem cell research internationally.

International Society for Stem Cell Research (ISSCR)
111 Deer Lake Rd., Suite 100, • Deerfield, Illinois 60015
(847) 509-1944 • fax: (847) 480-9282
e-mail: isscr@isscr.org • Web site: www.isscr.org

Formed in 2002, the ISSCR is an independent, nonprofit organization created to foster the exchange of information on stem cell research. It publishes a monthly newsletter called *The Pulse*, which provides the latest stem cell research news, schedules of scientific and industry meetings, and other general information useful to scientists working with stem cells. ISSCR is also affiliated with the award-winning journal *Cell Stem Cell*, a forum that covers a wide range of information about stem cell biology research.

Research! America

1101 King St., Suite 520, Alexandria, VA 22314-2960
(800) 366- 2873 • fax: (703) 739-2372
e-mail: info@researchamerica.org
Web site: www.researchamerica.org

Research! America is the nation's largest nonprofit public education and advocacy alliance representing more than five hundred medical, health, and scientific organizations. The goal is to improve awareness about the importance of scientific and medical research to the health of American citizens. It regularly conducts public opinion polls and publishes those results in its annual report called *America Speaks* and provides a monthly newsletter, *The Research Advocate*, which features articles about research funding, research in the news, and advocacy initiatives.

Bibliography

Books

Fox, Cynthia, *Cell of Cells: The Global Race to Capture and Control the Stem Cell*. New York: W.W. Norton, 2007.

Furcht, Leo, and William Hoffman, *The Stem Cell Debate: Beacons of Hope or Harbingers of Doom?* New York: Arcade, 2008.

George, Robert P., and Christopher Tollefsen, *Embryo: A Defense of Human Life*. New York: Doubleday, 2008.

Herold, Eve, *Stem Cell Wars: Inside Stories from the Frontlines*. New York: Palgrave Macmillan, 2007.

Perry, Yvonne, *Right to Recover: Winning the Political and Religious Wars over Stem Cell Research in America*. Mequon, WI: Nightengale, 2007.

Peters, Ted, *Sacred Cells? Why Christians Should Support Stem Cell Research*. Lanham, MD: Rowman & Littlefield, 2008.

Svendsen, Clive Niels, and Allison D. Ebert, eds., *Encyclopedia of Stem Cell Research*. Thousand Oaks, CA: Sage, 2008.

Yount, Lisa, *Biotechnology and Genetic Engineering: Library in a Book*. New York: Facts On File, 2008.

Periodicals and Internet Sources

Begley, Sharon, "Still No Truce in the Stem-Cell Wars," *Newsweek*, February 11, 2010.

Brown, Gordon, "Why I Believe Stem Cell Researchers Deserve Our Backing," *Guardian* (Manchester), May 18, 2008.

Brown, Judie, "We Deserve Better than Embryonic Stem Cell Research Fraud," Renew America, January 10, 2007.

Coalition of Americans for Ethical Research, "Two Major Studies Show: Human Pluripotent Stem Cells Without Cloning or Destroying Embryo," November 20, 2007.

Collins, Timothy P., "Why Does President Obama Object to Human Cloning?" *American Thinker*, March 22, 2009.

Devolder, Katrien, and Julian Savulescu, "A Defense of Stem Cell and Cloning Research," Oxford Uehiro Centre for Practical Ethics. www.practicalethics.ox.ac.uk/Pubs/Savulescu/stemcellresearch.pdf.

Epstein, Alex, "The Religious Right's Culture of Living Death," *Capitalism Magazine*, April 29, 2007.

Fumento, Michael, "The Dirty Secret of Embryonic Stem Cell Research," *Forbes*, July 15, 2009.

Healy, Bernadine, "Why Embryonic Stem Cells Are Obsolete," *U.S. News and World Report*, Marcy 4, 2009.

Jacoby, Jeff, "Embryos and Ethics," *Boston Globe*, March 15, 2009.

Keim, Brandon, "Bush Stem Cell Ban Wrong, but Not Anti-Science," *Wired*, March 11, 2009.

Kemp, Bob, "Embryonic Stem Cell Research: Bad Science Funded by the White House," Renew America.com, July 30, 2009.

Krauthammer, Charles, "Morally Unserious in the Extreme," RealClearPolitics, March 13, 2009.

Lopez, Kathryn, "Cloning by Any Other Name Is Still Cloning," *Jewish World Review*, June 12, 2007.

Masci, David, "The Case for Embryonic Stem Cell Research: An Interview with Jonathan Moreno," Pew Forum on Religion and Public Life, July 17, 2008.

Naab, Kathleen, interview with Father Alfred Cioffi, "When Stem Cell Research Gets Personal (Part I)," Zenit News Agency, June 9, 2009.

National Review, "Stem-Cell Success Story," November 21, 2007.

Obama, Barack, "Remarks of President Barack Obama—as Prepared for Delivery, Signing of Stem Cell Executive Order and Scientific Integrity Presidential Memorandum," March 9, 2009.

Park, Alice, "New Rules Expand Federal Funding of Stem Cells," *Time*, July 7, 2009.

Pew Forum on Religion and Public Life, "The Case Against Embryonic Stem Cell Research: An Interview with Yuval Levin," July 17, 2008.

Sandel, Michael J., "Embryo Ethics," *Boston Globe*, April 8, 2007.

Savulescu, Julian, "The Case for Creating Human-Nonhuman Cell Lines," Hastings Center, January 24, 2007.

Smith, Wesley J., "Cloning Doubletalk," *Weekly Standard*, March 26, 2007.

———, "Stem Cell Debate Is Over Ethics, Not Science," *Orthodoxy Today*, March 23, 2009.

Pence, Mike, "The Empty Promise of Embryonic Stem Cell Research," *Christianity Today*, March 23, 2009.

Trippi, Joe, "Science You Can Believe In," RealClearPolitics, March 13, 2009.

U.S. Department of Energy Office of Science, Office of Biological and Environmental Research, Human Genome Project, May 11, 2009.

Web Sites

National Institutes of Health Stem Cell Information Page (http://stemcells.nih.gov). This site, maintained by the National Institutes of Health, offers a solid primer for those seeking more information on stem cells and the debate surrounding them. Explains current U.S. policy on stem cell research in a clear and informative manner. The site also offers basic stem cell information, stem cell reports that review the state of research, a glossary, photos and illustrations, and links to related sources.

Stem Cells at the National Academies (http://dels .nas.edu/bls/stemcells). This site is maintained by the

National Academies, the federal government's advisory agency on science. It offers reports, brochures, and booklets on stem cells, cloning, and genetic engineering that can be downloaded for free.

University of Wisconsin Stem Cell & Regenerative Medicine Center (www.stemcells.wisc.edu/about .html). The University of Wisconsin's center for stem cell and regenerative medicine research and a leader in the field of stem cell research, the school was home to the world's first successful culturing of human embryonic stem cells. The mission of the center is to advance stem cell science through faculty, research efforts, and education.

Index

will not lead to human
cloning, 57–63
See also Embryonic
stem cell research
Stem cells
induced pluripotent,
42–45, 62
tissues derived from,
27
uses of, 24
See also Adult stem
cells; Embryonic stem
cells
Suleman, Nadya, 58

T
Thomas, E. Donnall, 46
Thomson, James, 40, 41, 45

U
United States Conference
of Catholic Bishops
(USCCB), 23–30, 33, 35

W
Wade, Nicholas, 37

Y
Yamanaka, Shinya, 37, 45

Picture Credits

About the Editor

Lauri S. Friedman earned her bachelor's degree in religion and political science from Vassar College in Poughkeepsie, New York. Her studies there focused on political Islam. Friedman has worked as a nonfiction writer, a newspaper journalist, and an editor for more than ten years. She has extensive experience in both academic and professional settings.

Friedman is the founder of LSF Editorial, a writing and editing business in San Diego. She has edited and authored numerous publications for Greenhaven Press on controversial social issues such as Islam, genetically modified food, women's rights, school shootings, gay marriage, and Iraq. Every book in the *Writing the Critical Essay* series has been under her direction or editorship, and she has personally written more than twenty titles in the series. She was instrumental in the creation of the series and played a critical role in its conception and development.